Loudoun County Virginia

Partially Proven Deeds

Patricia B. Duncan

HERITAGE BOOKS
2009

HERITAGE BOOKS
AN IMPRINT OF HERITAGE BOOKS, INC.

Books, CDs, and more—Worldwide

For our listing of thousands of titles see our website
at
www.HeritageBooks.com

Published 2009 by
HERITAGE BOOKS, INC.
Publishing Division
100 Railroad Ave. #104
Westminster, Maryland 21157

International Standard Book Numbers
Paperbound: 978-0-7884-4913-0
Clothbound: 978-0-7884-8146-8

Introduction

The following are abstracts of Partially Proven Deeds as appear in three parts or volumes available to the public at the courthouse in Leesburg. Part 1 consists of pages 1-346, Part 2 consists of pages 347-852 and Part three consists of pages 853-100153. These books contain photocopies of the original deeds, wills, and other documents and records. Because these are originals and not the clerk's recording in the court books, they are often in poor condition and difficult to read. Note that some of these deeds were later fully proven and were recorded in the regular Deed Books.

In addition to providing the basic information of book:page number, parties involved, and type of document, I have also included the date of the document, a brief description of the item, including adjourning neighbors, and witnesses. Information in italics was typed in margin of book. This was usually the information that was later recorded on the outside of the papers or additional remarks.

The microfilm (Reel 163) of these records available from the Library of Virginia Interlibrary Loan Service covers only pages 1-844. Copies of the documents may be obtained from the Office of Clerk of Circuit Court County of Loudoun, Box 550, Leesburg, VA 20178-0550.

Special thanks to the Library of Virginia and the Special Collections Library in Albuquerque, New Mexico, as well as John Fishback and Marty Hiatt for their help with this project.

Examples

BOOK 01 PAGE 105

This Indenture made & entered into this Twenty [illegible]th Day of Decem^r in the year of Our Lord one Thous[and] Eight Hundred & four Between Mary Evans Wido[w] of Wm Evans deceased of the one part & Wm Chick of the oth[er] part, Witnesseth that whereas the said Mary Evans hath Bargained Sold & conveyed unto the said Wm Chick all her right title & Interest — To which she hath in her deceased Hus[band's] Land — To Wit, Her Dower of the Lot whereon her Dec^d Husband Wm Evans Lived & Died upon — Called the Little Mountain Lot — & also her Dower of an other Lot Called By the name of the Indian Lick Lot — in the Will of Old John Evans — Together [with] all arrearages of every kind & nature appertaining to aforesaid premises — for and in consideration of the Sum of [illegible] pounds Lawfull Money of Virginia in hand paid by Wm Chick — The receipt whereof She doth hereby Acknowledge — This Conveyance to said Wm Chick only being for & During natural life of said Mary Evans, with all appurtenances [of] every kind & nature appertaining to the aforesaid Lot [of] Land for the only proper use & behoof of him the said Wm Chick his heirs & assigns, for & During the term [of] & the said Mary Evans do Covenant & agree for her self [her] heirs & assigns with the said Wm Chick his heirs & [assigns] to Warrant & defend the said Land & appurtenances unto said Wm Chick his heirs & assigns for & during her life against all & every person or persons whatever Claiming from or under her the said Mary Evans In testimony [whereof] The said Mary Evans have hereunto subscribed her [name] & affixed her Seal the day & year first written in the [illegible] of —

Mary Ev[ans]

Tested
Jno Latimer
Elisha Chick
Thomas Dun[illegible]

Partially Proven Deed 01:105

BOOK 01 PAGE 311

This Indenture made the twenty forth Day of April in the Year of our Lord one thousand seven hundred and ninety Nine Between Isaac Humphrey of the County of Loudoun & Commonwealth of Virginia of the one part & Thomas Humphrey of the said County & Commonwealth of the other Part Witnesseth that the said Isaac Humphrey for & in Consideration of the sum of five shillings [illegible] to him the said [illegible] in hand paid by the said Thomas Humphrey the receipt whereof he doth hereby acknowledge hath granted bargained and sold and by these presents doth bargain and sell unto the said Thomas Humphrey all [illegible] that tract or parcel of Land situate lying & being in the County of Loudoun aforesaid and bounded as followeth viz Beginning at a red Oak in the [illegible] Branch [illegible] Extending thence N° 56 E° [illegible] hundred & eighty five poles to a [illegible] oak Corner to [illegible] said survey thence S° 34 W° two hundred & fifty eight Poles to two [illegible] thence with the line N° 12 W° [illegible] hundred & twenty five Poles to the first station containing two hundred & twenty seven acres together with all houses [illegible] and all other appurtenances to the same belonging & the Reversion & Reversions Remainder & Remainders rents issues and profits of the same to have & to hold the same with the Appurtenances unto the said Thomas Humphrey his Ex. & Adm. from the [illegible] thereof for one year from thence next ensuing fully to be compleat and ended yielding and Paying therefore the Rent of one pepper Corn on the feast of St. Michael if demanded to the intent that by virtue hereof and of the Statute for Transferring uses into Possession the said Thomas Humphrey may be in actual Possession of the premises & be enabled to [illegible] a grant of the reversion and inheritance thereof to him and his heirs forever in witness whereof the said Isaac Humphrey hath hereunto set his hand & seal the Day and year above written

Isaac Humphrey

Sealed & Delivered in the presence of us

Thomas [illegible]

Samuel [illegible]

[illegible] Newton

Partially Proven Deed 01:311

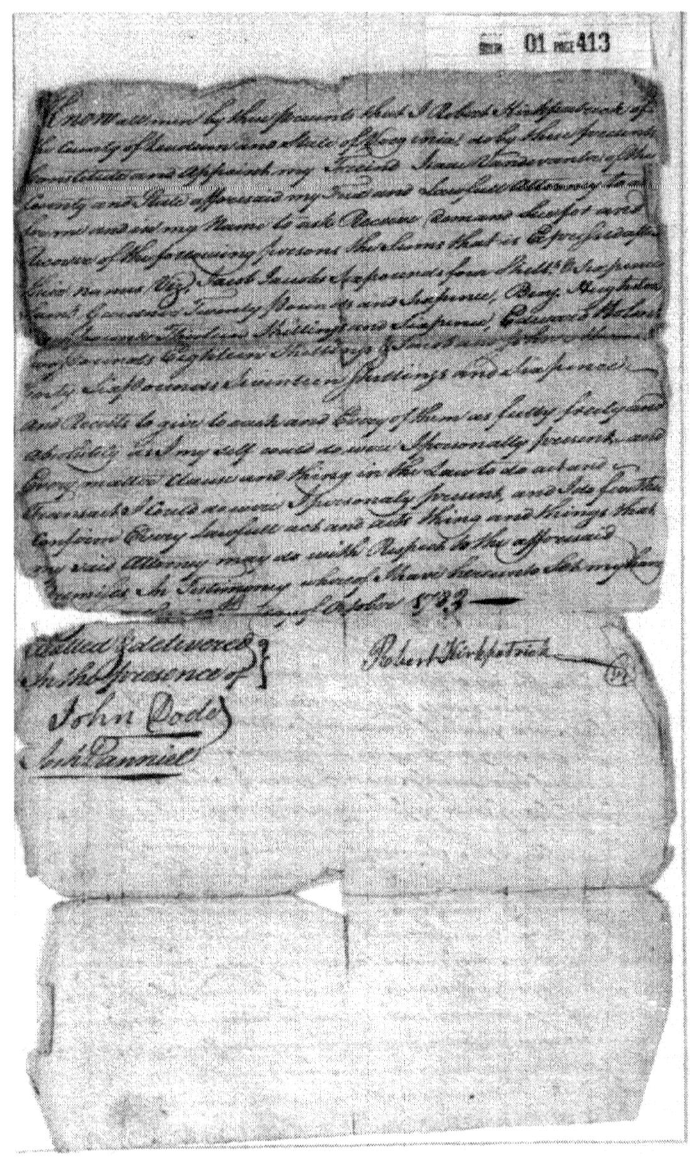

BOOK 01 PAGE 413

Know all men by these presents that I Robert Kirkpatrick of
the County of Loudoun and State of Virginia do by these presents
Constitute and Appoint my Friend [illegible] of the
County and State aforesaid my true and Lawfull Attorney for
me and in my Name to ask Receive demand sue for and
Recover of the following persons the sums that is Expressed against
their names Viz. Jacob [illegible] pounds four Shill.s & Sixpence
[illegible] Twenty pounds and Sixpence, Benj. [illegible]
[illegible] Thirteen Shillings and Sixpence, [illegible]
[illegible] Eighteen Shillings & [illegible]
[illegible] Seventeen Shillings and Sixpence
and Receits to give to each and Every of them as fully freely and
absolutely as I my self could do were I personally present and
Every matter Cause and thing in the Law to do act and
transact as I could do were I personally present, and I do further
Confirm Every Lawfull act and all thing and things that
my said Attorney may do with Respect to the aforesaid
premises In Testimony whereof I have hereunto set my hand
[illegible] day of October [illegible]

Signed Sealed and Delivered
In the presence of
John Dodd
[illegible]

Robert Kirkpatrick (Seal)

Partially Proven Deed 01:413

BOOK 01 PAGE 491

Know all Men by these Presents that I Israel Lacey of the County of Loudoun in consideration of the friendship I bear towards Letty Palmer of said County, have lent to the said Letty Palmer the following Property to wit: four head of Cattle, one sow and five Hogs two ploughs & gears, two beds and bedding three bedsteads, one Sleigh and all the household & Kitchen furniture now in sd Palmers Possession

and by these Presents do lend the said property to the said Palmer, to hold during my will and Pleasure and I do hereby expressly declare that sd Palmer [illegible] power to [illegible] said Property whenever I choose and I do moreover declare that if I die without recalling said Property or any part thereof from said Palmer that said Loan is to cease immediately upon my death and the said Property to revert to my Executors subject to the provisions of my Will, or in the event of my intestacy to my Administrators. Given under my hand & Seal this 8 day of March 1814

Signed Sealed & delivered in presence of

Israel Lacey (Seal)

[illegible]
John Hendricks
[illegible]

Partially Proven Deed 01:491

BOOK 01 PAGE 797

Know all Men, by these presents, That I
Charles Smith of the County of Loudoun
and State of Virginia, for and in Consideration of the Sum of Five Hundred Dollars
Lawful money of Virginia, to me in Hand
paid, by Winniford Smith of the afforsaid
County and State, the Receipt whereof I
do hereby acknowledge, have bargaind, sold
and deliverd. and by these Presents, according to the due Form of Law, do bargain,
sell and deliver unto the said Winniford-
Smith the Following Negroes &c. Silvy,
Harry, Rachel, Ellick, Sarah and Matilda
Sealed up by Consent with my Seal. To
have and to hold the said Negroes unto
the sd Winniford Smith and her Heirs forever
and I the sd Charles Smith shall and will warrant, and forever defend the afforsaid Negroes from me my Heirs or Executors: in Witness whereof, I have hereto set my Hand and Seal
This Twentieth day of November in the
Year of our Lord 1799.

Test
Wm Coleman
Thos Coleman

Charles Smith (Seal)

Partially Proven Deed 01:797

PARTIALLY PROVEN DEEDS

Bk:Pg: 01:01 Date: 8 February 1845
E. M. ANDERSON and C. F. ANDERSON to Abner GIBSON Sheriff of Loudoun. Now confined in custody of Sheriff at the suit of O. C. Tiffany & Co. and desirous to be discharged; conveys title and interest in schedule delivered per relief of insolvent debtors.

Bk:Pg: 01:02 – 01:03 Date: 1 September 1828
Michael ARNOLD to Benjamin LESLIE. Transfer of water rights from the spring which runs through ARNOLD's land to LESLIE's tanyard. Witness: John A. MARMADUKE, Evan EVANS, Mahlon RUSSELL. *Proven by Evan EVANS 11 March 1833.*

Bk:Pg: 01:03 – 01:04 Date: 20 September 1823
Thomas BUCK of Frederick Va and Reuhamah McKIM of Loudoun. Marriage agreement – property shall remain property of party now holding it. Conveys dwelling houses, out houses, garden, and orchards and $200/yr to Reuhamah during her natural life. Witness: Andrew HEATH, Robert LATHAM, Abel JAMES. *Proven by Abel JAMES on 13 Oct. 1823 and Andrew HEATH 26 July 1824.*

Bk:Pg: 01:04 Date: 19 April 1833
James BROWN to Isaac BROWN (as agent in fact for John BROWN). Note for $550.37½ for purchase of land on 1 March 1831 and being part of the surplus after paying NICHOLS debt for which the land was sold, to be paid by 1 September 1836. Witness: Joseph J. BROWN, Thornton WALKER, Felix TRIPLETT. *Proven by Thornton WALKER 10 Oct. 1833 and Felix TRIPLETT 26 March 1834.*

Bk:Pg: 01:05 Date: 19 April 1833
James BROWN to Isaac BROWN Sr. (as agent in fact for John BROWN). Note for $550.37½ for land purchased 1 March 1831 and being part of the surplus after paying NICHOLS debt for which the land was sold, to be paid by 1 September 1836. Witness: Joseph J. BROWN, Thornton WALKER, Felix TRIPLETT. *Proven by Thornton WALKER 10 Oct. 1833 and Felix TRIPLETT 26 March 1834.* [This note is repeated twice on this page. Typed in at bottom of second entry – *As appears on the back, 1834 – I do hereby bind myself to pay the interest on the within note annually. Signed James BROWN*]

Bk:Pg: 01:06 Date: 19 April 1833
James BROWN to Isaac BROWN Sr. (as agent in fact for John BROWN). Note for $550.37½ for land purchased 1 March 1831 and being part of the surplus after paying NICHOLS debt for which the

land was sold, to be paid by 1 September ___. Witness: Joseph J. BROWN, Thornton WALKER, Felix TRIPLETT. *Proven by Thornton WALKER 10 Oct. 1833 and Felix TRIPLETT 26 March 1834*. [typed in at bottom – *As appears on the back. I do hereby bind myself to pay the interest on the within note annually. Signed: James BROWN*]

Bk:Pg: 01:07 Date: 8 March 1849

William N. BERKLEY of Loudoun to William B. COCHRAN and Francis W. POWELL of Loudoun. Bargain and sale of 187¾a on south side of Little River Turnpike Road (conveyed as gift on 19 October 1848 from Lewis BERKELEY & wife to William) adj ___ JAMES. [no witness signatures] Acknowledged by BERKELEY 8 March 1849 before John MOORE and Hugh SMITH Justices of the Peace of Loudoun.

Bk:Pg: 01:09 Date: 10 December 1799

Report of road petitioned for by Airis BUCKNER from Neal's corner on the turnpike road to Debell's ford on Bull Run is returned as follows: to run starting the line of land formerly belonging to William LEE Esqr. of Greenspring until it comes to Airis BUCKNER's land thence through the said BUCKNER's land to his fence, thence along his fence a straight line to the end thence the most straight & convenient way to the lower end of the Beaver Dam on bull run, thence down the run which is the line to the estate of John CARTER Esqr. dec'd to Debell's ford. Writ of summon issue to Robert CARTER for himself & as agent for the heirs of John CARTER dec'd, William HODGSON and Richard Bland LEE Guardian of Miss Cornelia LEE to appear here at the next court to show why said road should not be opened accordingly. Signed C. BINNS, Clk.

Bk:Pg: 01:10 Date: ___

Eliz'th BARTON, Jos. BARTON, Jno. BARTON, Thos. BARTON, Jos. LOVE, Saml. BROHARD & wife in division ret'd & not recorded. No. 2.

Gideon HOUSHOLDER, Solomon HOUSHOLDER, David AXLINE & Daniel HOUSHOLDER report of division ret'd. No. 2.

Division of SNOOTS land (Jacob SPRINGS & Anthony FAWLEY). Report of division ret'd No. 2.

Jno. VANHORN land divided rep't ret'd. No. 3

Jno. VIOLETT's land &c divided. No. 3.

BUTCHER & OVERFIELD &c report & ret'd. No. 4

POWELL vs POWELL &c No. 4, nothing done.

DILLY & wife – EVANS report ret'd. No. 5.

LANE &c JETT report ret'd No. 5.

Caruthers & Caruthers &c report ret'd No. 6.

TRIBBY & TRIBY &c report ret'd No. 6.

CLAGETT to HOLMES trustee about 20 years
d^{o} to CARR trustee about 15 d^{o}
d^{o} to Thos. SWANN's trustee d^{o} d^{o}
see if deed of trust & then if deed of release.
1837 June 5 1st payment, G. H. LUCKETT

Bk:Pg: 01:11 Date: 15 December 1769

Hezekiah BOON of Loudoun to Farling BALL of Loudoun. Note of £15.11.0 in penal sum of £15.11.0. Witness: Jno. HARYFORD.

Bk:Pg: 01:12 Date: 4 September 1832

Flavius J. BRADEN of Natchez, Miss. to William BURCHETT of Loudoun. Bill of sale for negro man James MITCHELL aged about 46y, dark complexion, about 5"9. Witness: Noble S. BRADEN. *Proven by Nobel S. BRADEN 30 Jan. 1836.*

Bk:Pg: 01:13 – 01:14 Date: 29 October 1831

Noble S. BRADEN Exor. of Robert BRADEN dec'd and Peter COST of Loudoun of the first part, John BAKER late of this county but now of state of Ohio of second part and Jacob COST of Loudoun of third part. Release of interest in several tracts - John BAKER on 3 May 1821 made trust to secure payment of $4,590 to Jacob COST, now fully satisfied. Witness: Joshua OSBURN as to Jacob COST. *Nov. 14, 1831 acknowledged by Peter COST & N. S. BRADEN, Exor.*

Bk:Pg: 01:15 – 01:16 Date: 28 January 1841

Baley/Bailey BARTON & wife Sarah of Loudoun of first part, William G. LEITH of Loudoun of second part and James M. BENTON of Loudoun of the third part. BARTON made bond of $105 using undivided interest in land of James WORNAL dec'd supposed to be about 18a (Sarah's share at the death of her mother). To pay in full on 1 January next. Acknowledged 28 January 1841 by Baley with certificate of examination for Sarah signed by Ludwell LUCKETT & William BENTON Justices of Loudoun. *1841 Feby 2nd rec'd.*

Bk:Pg: 01:17 Date: 17 March 1825

Norval CHAMBLIN to Wm. J. BRONAUGH. Trust for benefit of Price JACOBS (sold him 33 acres but Norval's wife under age of 21 years) using negro boy named Richard age about 12 years. Witness: Wm. BRONAUGH, David GALLEHER. *Proven by William BRONAUGH 8 August 1825.*

Bk:Pg: 01:18 – 01:19 Date: 28 April 1810

John S. CRANWELL of Leesburg to William WRIGHT of Leesburg. Bargain and sale of Lot. No. 40 in Leesburg (purchased of Capt. Wm. TAYLOR of Leesburg in Oct. last, deed and trust recorded last

Feb). WRIGHT agrees to pay TAYLOR sum agreed between CRANWELL and TAYLOR, exonerating CRANWELL of any interest. Witness: C. BINNS, Isaac LAROWE, Saml. M. EDWARDS.

Bk:Pg: 01:20 Date: ___

Printed form for private examination of wife of John S. CRANWELL. No other information filled in. Signed C. BINNS.

Bk:Pg: 01:21 – 01:22 Date: 5 April 1821

Joseph CARR of Loudoun to Stephen REED & Mandley IDEN of Loudoun. Lease of ½a in Upperville on south side of main street or turnpike road adj John JAMES' shop lot, Joshua HARDY. Witness: C. B. POLLARD, Caldwell CARR, John JAMES, John FLEMING, Burr G. POWELL. *Proven 10 June 1822 by Caldwell CARR before me, Jno. A. BINNS, D.C. Proven 8 Aug. 1826 by John FLEMING before me, Jno. A. BINNS, D.C.*

Bk:Pg: 01:23 Date: 30 March 1827

Edmund CAMMACK and Thos. N. LANGSTON. Release of claim upon estate of Stacy HAINS dec'd by deed of trust given by HAYNES in which John M. McCARTY is trustee dated 1 August 1824. Witness: Joseph HOGUE, Nathan ODEN.

Bk:Pg: 01:24 – 01:25 Date: 22 May 1806

Richard CROSS of Loudoun to Anthony LUCAS of Loudoun. Mortgage of $300 using farm animals, farm and household items. Witness: Fleet SMITH, Tho. SWANN.

Bk:Pg: 01:26 Date: 14 April 1812

Susannah/Susan CHILTON of Loudoun and Saml. CLAPHAM of Loudoun to Thomas SANDS of Loudoun and Andrew M. BIRDSALL of Loudoun. Bond for $1,400 using 182½a purchased by Capt. Thomas CHILTON dec'd of Saml. CLAPHAM adj. S. CLAPHAM and Thomas NOLAND dec'd. Witness: Geo. W. BALL as to S. CLAPHAM. William BIRDSALL. *Proven 14 Dec. 1812 by William BIRDSALL.*

Bk:Pg: 01:27 Date: ___ 1825

William CARR of Loudoun to Henson Townsend MONROE son of Henson MONROE. Deed of gift of household items and bridle and saddle purchased at the sale of effects of Henson MONROE taken by distress to satisfy a rent due. [no signature or witnesses] *14 March 1825 acknowledged and admitted to record.*

Bk:Pg: 01:28 Date: 11 January 1825

List of Henson MONROE's property sold to satisfy Wm. CARR, 11 Jany. 1825: farm animals, horse, household items, bridle & saddle, totaling $28.13. Signed Everitt SANDERS, Const. Hen. Townsend MONROE written at bottom.

Bk:Pg: 01:29 – 01:32 Date: 7 August 1824

John H. CASSADY of Loudoun to David SHAWEN of Loudoun. Trust for benefit of Henry HAINES of Charlestown, Jefferson County, Va in debt of $1,590 to be paid by 1 August 1825, using interest in 284a (willed to him by Nancy McGEATH dec'd), adj. Stephen DANIEL, William WRIGHT, ___ THOMPSON. Witness: Noble S. BRADEN, Wm. FITZIMMONS, Jesse GOVER. *11 December 1826 acknowledged by SHAWEN and proven by William FITZIMMONS as to CASSADY. 9 Jan. 1827 proven by Noble S. BRADEN.*

Bk:Pg: 01:33 – 01:35 Date: 19 August 1817

Joseph CARR of Loudoun to Thomas W. SMITH of Loudoun. Bargain and sale of 1a in Upperville (part of 31¾a conveyed by Stephen McPHERSON dec'd), adj SMITH, turnpike road. Witness: Caldwell CARR, John JAMES, Joshua HARDY, Jacob IDEN. *Proven 14 February 1838 by Caldwell CARR.*

Bk:Pg: 01:36 – 01:37 Date: 22 May 1823

Ozzias/Ozias CRAMPTON of Frederick Co. Md attorney-in-fact for Josias CRAMPTON of Frederick Co. Md to William McMAKIN of Frederick Co. Md. Bill of sale of female negro slaves Kitty about age 11y and Eliza about 5y old now in possession of John MOORE of Loudoun. Witness: John MOORE. *Proven by John MOORE 24 May 1823.*

Bk:Pg: 01:38 Date: 10 July 1809

Sheriff to take possession of the estate of Obadiah CLIFFORD deceased and make sale. On back states that *Charles ELGIN, Deputy Sheriff of O. BENNETT, Sheriff applied to ___ CLIFFORD for the property of Obidiah CLIFFORD who states that he had left none and no property that he know of.*

Bk:Pg: 01:39 – 01:40 Date: 10 April 1823

Joseph CARR of Upperville to John HARDY of Upperville. Lease (first payment due 1 January 1824) of ½a lot in Upperville lately in occupation of William FULKERSON on south side of turnpike road. Witness: Caldwell CARR, John JAMES John KIMBER. *Proven 27 August 1823 by Caldwell CARR.*

Bk:Pg: 01:41 – 01:43 Date: 19 May 1810

James CAMPBELL & wife Ruth of Loudoun to William CLAYTON [Sr. on cert. of exam.] of Loudoun. Bargain and sale of 15a on side of Blue Ridge being part of land obtained by virtue of a land office treasury warrant No. 2244 issued 9 August 1797 adj lane leading to the Mountain and adj William Ludwell LEE. Witness: Martin OVERFIELD, George Hawkins ALLDER, John BRARDY. Certificate of examination of wife dated 13 October 1810 returned by Stacy TAYLOR and Notley C. WILLIAMS. [*Recorded Deed Book 2M:328*]

Bk:Pg: 01:44 – 01:45 Date: 13 October 1810

James CAMPBELL & wife Ruth of Loudoun to William McFARLING of Loudoun. Bargain and sale of 25a (part of tract granted CAMPBELL 6 March 1809) adj William L. LEE. Witness: George Hawkins ALDER, John BRARDY, Edward CUNARD Jr. *Proven 11 December 1810 by George Hawkins ALLDER and John BRARDY. (See also page 01:52)*

Bk:Pg: 01:46 - 01:48 Date: 5 [torn] 1788

Patrick CAVAN to William WILSON of Fairfax Va. Mortgage on ½a Lots No. 6 and 59 in Leesburg. Witness: Robert HART?, Isaac LARROWE, George NELSON. *Proven 13 May 1800 by Isaac LARROWE one of the subscribing witness thereto.*

Bk:Pg: 01:49 – 01:51 Date: 17 January 1817

Joseph CIMMINGS & wife Mary of Loudoun to George RUST Jr. of Loudoun. Bargain and sale of 54a adj LACEY (conveyed by Thos. CIMMINGS to Joseph 8 June 1812, Deed Book 2P, page 88) and 2 other lots (conveyed by John NIXON & wife Jane dated 9 December 1816) being 29a lot No. 1 in division of estate of Tho. CIMMINGS dec'd which descended to his daughter Jane and the latter 1½a. Witness: George SWEARINGEN, Josias CLAPHAM, Saml. M. EDWARDS. *Proven 12 April 1818 by George SWEARINGEN.*

Bk:Pg: 01:52 Date: 13 October 1810

Certificate of examination for bargain and sale by James CAMPBELL & wife Ruth to William McFARLING for 25a. Returned by Stacy TAYLOR and N. C. WILLIAMS. *[also see page 01:44*]

Bk:Pg: 01:53 – 01:56 Date: 13 Jul 1822

Hiland CROWE of Loudoun to Charles LEWIS and John BAYLY [*Amos SKINNER's trustees* typed in margin] of Loudoun. Bargain and sale of 71a adj Ball's corner, John SPENCER, J. BINNS, Mary STOKES. Witness: S. BLINCOE, John DRISH, Martin CORDELL. Proven by S. BLINCOE and Jonathan DRISH 30 April 1824. If Amos SKINNER should have to pay the judgment obtained by

Elizabeth A. HOLSTEIN against him in an action of detinue brought by her in Superior Court of Loudoun to recover a Negroe boy Charles, then Hiland will owe SKINNER $200 with interest from 2 June 1819 that LEWIS and BAYLY will sell Negroe to pay. Witness: S. BLINCOE, John DRISH, Martin CORDELL. *Proven 30 April 1824 by S. BLINCOE & Jno. DRISH.*

Bk:Pg: 01:57 – 01:59 Date: 16 February 1811
Samuel MURRAY, Armistead LONG and William CHILTON trustees of Obadiah CLIFFORD & wife Betsey to Charles BINNS of Loudoun. Bargain and sale of all land lying between Loudoun & Royal Streets purchased of Daniel DOWLING & wife & from HAMBLETON's representatives (26 November 1806 CLIFFORD executed deed of trust) and houses occupied by CLIFFORD and J. T. MASON Jr. Witness: Saml. M. EDWARDS, Dr. S. GRAY, Isaac LAROWE, Chs. ELGIN, Daniel GRAY. *Proven by S. MURRAY and William CHILTON on 13 May 1811.*

Bk:Pg: 01:60 – 01:61 Date: 31 October 1797
John CAMELL/CAMPBELL of Loudoun to Mortho SULLIVAN of Loudoun. Bargain and sale of 60a on main road leading from Leesburg to Alexandria adj Wm. B'd. PAGE; to be paid by 31 October 1798 with legal interest. Witness: C. BINNS Jr., Alex'r. WAUGH, Thos. FOUCH.

Bk:Pg: 01:62 Date: 10 March 1811
Rec'd of Clerk of Loudoun a deed exc'd 14 April 1802 by Rich'd. COLEMAN & wife Elizabeth to me. Signed Alexander YOUNG.

Bk:Pg: 01:63 – 01:65 Date: 19 May 1810
James CAMPBELL of Loudoun to Tholemiah RHODES of Loudoun. Bargain and sale of 10a near Blue Ridge part of larger tract CAMPBELL obtained by land office Treasury Warrant No. 2244 issued 9 August 1797, adj BROOKE and OVERFIELD, Wm. L. LEE. Witness: Martin OVERFIELD, George Hawkins ALLDER, John BRARDY. Includes small plat. *Proven 10 December 1810 by George Hawkins ALDER and John BRARDY.*

Bk:Pg: 01:66 Date: 15 October 1808
Sarah CRAVEN Administratrix of Abner CRAVEN dec'd of Loudoun to friend Aaron SANDERS. Power of Attorney for business of intestate deceased husband. Witness: Isaac LAROWE, Eli OFFUTT.

Bk:Pg: 01:67 – 01:68 Date: 15 February 1804
Examination of Sarah wife of Nathaniel CRAWFURD for sale of 177a to William CARTER Loudoun by Samuel HEPBURN and David CRAWFURD of Prince Georges Co. Md.

Bk:Pg: 01:69 Date: 15 September 1824
Samuel COOKE to James H. COOKE. Assignment of all household and kitchen furniture (list of items) to be sold to pay balance of rent the amount not known to William WIRE, $190 to Peter STUCK, with excess to use of James H. COOKE. Witness: Alex'r. CORDELL, Whiting COOKE. *Proven 21 December 1824 by Whiting COOKE.*

Bk:Pg: 01:70 – 01:72 Date: 22 February 1803
Alexander COUPAR & wife Margaret of Leesburg to Peter DOW of Loudoun. Trust using Margaret's 1/5th share of estate of Robert HAMILTON dec'd late of Loudoun. Witness: Jas. CAVAN Jr., George HAMMAT, Samuel LINDSAY, Robt. HAMILTON, Nancy COOPER, Josh'a BAKER. *Proven 10 May 1804 by James CAVAN Jr. and George HAMMAT.*

Bk:Pg: 01:73 – 01:74 Date: 17 April 1790
Joseph COMBS of Loudoun to Rawleigh COLSTON of Frederick Co. Va. Bargain and sale of 5a adj Charles WEST and mill on Goose Creek the property of COLSTON. Witness: Alex. MARSHALL, Burr POWELL, Lucy MARSHALL. *Proven 14 August 1809 by Burr POWELL.*

Bk:Pg: 01:75 – 01:76 Date: 19 November 1827
Samuel CARR of Leesburg to Burr W. HARRISON of Leesburg. Trust for debt to John and James POGUE of Baltimore using one four wheeled carriage and three horses. Witness: Chs. G. ESKRIDGE, Alfred A. ESKRIDGE, Jas. L. HAMILTON.

Bk:Pg: 01:77 – 01:78 Date: 10 October 1804
William CHILTON and Alex'r SUTHERLAND. Agreement for sale of 49a (after deducting 1a sold to Obediah CLIFFORD and includes purchase from Joseph BENTLY for which SUTHERLAND agrees to pay) CHILTON purchased of George CARTER's Exors. Witness: A. LONG, Wm. H. HARDING, S'n. BLINCOE.

Bk:Pg: 01:79 Date: __ December 1807
Samuel CRAIG agent for Oats & Highley of Leeds in England to John HUTCHISON and Joshua HUTCHISON. Bargain and sale to John of 132a and Joshua of 46a (part of tract purchased from and mortgaged by Samuel LOVE to Oats & Highley which bonds were assigned by Charles J. LOVE to CRAIG). Bonds were paid off and

land being sold should be released. Witness: W. SETTLE, Henson GOWEN, Tho. MUSTEN. *Proven by William LITTLE and Hinson GOWEN on 11 January 1808.*

Bk:Pg: 01:80 – 01:81 Date: 17 May 1804
Jonathan CUNARD of Loudoun to John NICKLIN Sr. of Loudoun. Trust for debt to John NICKLIN Jr. using 50¾a purchased of John Jr. Witness: James HAMILTON, Isaac HOUGH, F. BALL. *Proven by James HAMILTON and Isaac HOUGH 10 December 1804.*

Bk:Pg: 01:82 – 01:83 Date: 7 September 1811
Eden CARTER & wife Susannah, John HANN & wife Ann and David NEWLON & wife Mary (heirs of Peter HANN dec'd) of Loudoun to George MARKS of Loudoun. Bargain and sale of 37a (part of tract Peter HANN dec'd held by deed from PHILIPS) nr Marks's Mill road. Witness: William HANN, Joshua OSBURN, N. C. WILLIAMS, Thomas BOTTS. *Acknowledged 9 September 1811 by Eden and Susannah CARTER. Proven by William HANN as to HANN and NEWLON 9 September 1811.*

Bk:Pg: 01:84 – 01:88 Date: 8 March 1804
Alexander COUPER & wife Margaret of Loudoun to Obadiah CLIFFORD of Loudoun. Trust for debt to Stephen DONALSON using interest to real and personal estate left by Robert HAMILTON dec'd (Margaret entitled to 1/5th of estate). Witness: Alexander COUPER Junr., B'd. HOUGH, Jas. HAMILTON. *Proven by Alexander COOPER Jur. and James HAMILTON 8 October 1804*

Bk:Pg: 01:89 – 01:90 Date: 14 March 1809
Suit in chancery some time ago Anthony CUNNARD & wife and others representatives of John CLISE dec'd against John CLISE Jr. Admr. of said John dec'd for their portion of estate. John Jr. sued CUNNARD &c. Now agreed between the parties that suit be entered as agreed. John CLISE doth release and forever quit claim any interest he may have in lease of 200a granted by George W. FAIRFAX to John dec'd in his lifetime in the neighborhood of Dinah BEEZER and Ebenezer GRUB to said Anthony CUNNARD & wife. Witness: S. BLINCOE, Edward CUNARD, John MATHEWS. *Proven by Sampson BLINCOE 9 October 1809.*

Bk:Pg: 01:91 Date: 6 May 1789
Vallentine CRONTZ of Loudoun to Henry TRUCKS. Assignment of lease of tenements and land purchased of Alex. COOPER lying on Tuskorora Run in Loudoun, formerly rented by Wm. COCKS. Witness: Pat'k. CAVAN, William BOOKES [BROOKS?]. *Proven 9 June 1789 by Patrick CAVAN and William BROOKS.*

Bk:Pg: 01:92 – 01:93 Date: 12 Jul 1844
Bailey D. COCKRILL to Abner OSBURN Sheriff of Loudoun. COCKRILL in custody on execution by John ISH and execution by Archibald N. DOUGLASS and intends to take oath of insolvent. Bargain and sale of 61¼a (purchased of Thomas BROWN 15 January 1840, Deed Book 4N, page 256). [*no witnesses nor proven*]

Bk:Pg: 01:94 – 01:95 Date: ___
Mahlon CRAVEN and Eli IDEN of Knox Co. Ohio to Henry TAYLOR of Loudoun. Power of attorney to receive from Thomas ONEALE of Loudoun amt. of decree from chancery suit. Witness: S. W. FAIGAHAN, A. C. ELLIOTT, Wm. DUNBAR. Acknowledged before Samuel W. FAIGAHAN clerk of Knox Co. Ohio dated 14 November 1848.

Bk:Pg: 01:96 – 01:99 Date: 3 August 1802
Thomas CHINN & wife Sarah of Loudoun to Robert CHINN of Loudoun. Bargain and sale of 200a adj ___ HALE, ___ RECTOR, ___ POWELL, Thomas CHINN. Includes a 25a lot conveyed by Thomas to Rich'd CHINN dated 26 June 1800 (deed never recorded) which Richard devised in will to Robert. To pay £20 each year as long as Thomas & Sarah live. Witness: Burr POWELL, Ralph MURRAY, Henry BRAWNER, Richard CRUPPER, Elijah CRUPPER. Reacknowledged 11 March 1804 witnessed by Burr POWELL, Saml. BOGGESS, John UPP. *Proven by Burr POWELL 12 September 1802 and John UPP 9 September 1816.*

Bk:Pg: 01:100 – 01:101 Date: 24 February 1847
Mary FRYE widow of Michael FRYE dec'd. Acknowledgement of personal property received from Exors. of dec'd husband. Gives list of household items and their value, totaling $1413.25. Witness: John GRUBB, Jerome W. GOODHART. (*Note on back of writing - 11 April 1851 "not to be recorded until it is proven by one of the witnesses and Mr. JANNEY thinks not to be recorded at all. A. S. N." Margin note – unproved by witnesses.*)

Bk:Pg: 01:102 – 01:104 Date: 18 March 1814
Bertrand EWELL of Loudoun of 1st part, Charles ALEXANDER & Charles TUTT of Loudoun of 2nd part and Catharine Barnes EWELL of Loudoun. Marriage contract made 4 October 17_8 [hole in paper, 1798 in marriage records] gave Bertrand certain slaves and other property in trust for use by Catharine and her children. Bertrand sold those negroes as well as negroes Tom, Billy, Sophy & Gurdy which Jno. ALEXANDER gave to the sole use of Catharine & children which Catharine consented to. John ALEXANDER on 5 November

1806 conveyed to Bertrand a parcel of land for Bertrand to prosecute in Chancery for land in the cause between ALEXANDER & a certain CLEVELAND & others and after case is done and Bertrand paid 1/3 of residue to go to daughter Penelope Barnes ALEXANDER and the residue to daughter Catharine B. EWELL & her children. Trust land includes 519a, No. 38 in Township No. 2, the south next quarter section No. 35 in township No. 2 of Range No. 2 containing 162a, the southwest quarter of section No. 25 in Township No. 2 of range No. 2 containing 157a, the south east quarter of No. 25 in township No. 2 range No. 2 east containing 157a. Also all interest of Bertrand in estate of his dec'd father Jesse EWELL. Witness: Francis TRIPLETT Jr., William ELLIOTT, Felix McCARTY. *Acknowledged by B. EWELL 10 October 1814.*

Bk:Pg: 01:105 Date: 29 December 1804

Mary EVANS widow of of Wm. EVANS dec'd to Wm. CHICK. Bargain and sale of all her interest in dower lot where her dec'd husband lived & died called "Little Mountain Lot" and her dower of lot called "Indian Lick Lot" from the will of old John EVANS during her natural life. Witness: Thos. LATIMER, Elisha CHICK, Henson DUTY. *Proven by Thomas LATIMER and Elisha CHUCK [*CHICK*] 9 September 1805.*

Bk:Pg: 01:106 Date: 14 September 1829

Rec'd of Mr. C. BINNS a deed of trust Daniel EACHES to Saml. SINGLETON & Joshua HOGUE trustees for Samuel & Joseph HATCHER which is not recorded. Signed Thomas ROGERS Admr. of Samuel HATCHER, surviving partner of Saml. & Joseph HATCHER.

Bk:Pg: 01:107 – 01:108 Date: 3 September 1813

Lewis ELZEY of Loudoun of 1st part, James H. HAMILTON, George S. HOUGH & Thomas HOUGH of Loudoun of 2nd part and William HARNED of Loudoun of 3rd part. Release of trust by parties of 2nd part - Deed of trust dated August 1807 and now of record from William HARNED to HAMILTON, HOUGH & HOUGH for benefit of ELZEY conveying house and lot in Hillsborough formerly the property of John JANNEY dec'd and after his death sold to James BRADFIELD and by him sold to ELZEY, then conveyed by trust to HARNED. Witness: Stacy TAYLOR, Robert CUMMINGS, Abner OSBURN, George GIDEON, Thomas KIDWELL, Jesse DODD, Thos. McCOWAT, Henry H. HAMILTON, Thos. P. KNOX, Absolum COCKERILL, Saml. COCKERILL. *Proven by Thomas KIDWELL, Absolom COCKERILL, Samuel COCKERILL as to Lewis ELLZEY. Acknowledged 13 June 1814 by James H. HAMILTON and proven by Henry H. HAMILTON to act and deed of George S. HOUGH. Acknowledged 8 May 1815 by Thomas HOUGH.*

Bk:Pg: 01:109 – 01:110 Date: __th December 1828

Samuel M. EDWARDS of 1st part, Robert BENTLEY and John J. HARDING of 2nd part and Richard H. LEE of 3rd part, all of Loudoun. Release of trust from LEE dated 5 June 1824 for debt to BENTLEY & HARDING using house and lot in Leesburg. *10 December 1828 acknowledged by Sl. M. EDWARDS & R. H. LEE.*

Bk:Pg: 01:111 – 01:112 Date: 6 February 1798

Elizabeth ELLZEY & Mary ELLZEY of Loudoun to David DAVIS of Fairfax. Bargain and sale of 20¾a on Beaverdam being part of tract granted to Lewis ELLZEY by patent of 12 December 1740, adj Elizabeth & Mary, ___ LEE, Landon CARTER. Witness: John WHITELY, John SPENCER, W. ELLZEY, Thomas BEVERIDGE. *Proven 14 May 1798 by M. ELLZEY.*

Bk:Pg: 01:113 – 01:115 Date: 6 February 1798

Elizabeth ELLZEY & Mary ELLZEY of Loudoun to David DAVIS of Fairfax. Bargain and sale of 98a on Beaverdam (being part of tract granted Lewis ELLZEY by patent dated 12 December 1740) adj Elizabeth & Mary, ___ PILE. Witness: John WHITELY, John SPENCER, W. ELLZEY, Thomas BEVERIDGE. Proven 14 May 1798 by W. ELLZEY. *Proven 14 May 1798 by M. ELLZEY.*

Bk:Pg: 01:116 – 01:118 Date: 25 June 1800

William ELZEY & wife Frances Hill of Loudoun to Philip Richard FENDALL and Robert YOUNG of Alexandria Va. Patent land of 20,000a granted to Matthew ROBERTSON of Amelia Co. situated in Clark Co. Kentucky. Power of attorney from ROBERTSON to George GRAHAM now of Dumfries who conveyed land to ELZEY. Bargain and sale of 10,000a. Witness: Joseas YOUNG, Walt JONES Jr., Wm. H. RICE. Certificate of examination for Frances Hill dated 13 August 1800 returned by A. RUSSEL, Stacy TAYLOR.

Bk:Pg: 01:119 – 01:123 Date: 10 March 1812

Lewis ELLZEY & wife Rozannah of Loudoun of 1st part, Samuel Nichols & Co. of 2nd part and James HEATON & Joshua OSBURN of 3rd part, all of Loudoun. Trust for debt to Nichols & Co. using 128a formerly in possession of Francis FERGUSON held under a lease for lives adj Elizabeth REID, Solomon DAVIS, Thos. GREGG; 94a formerly held by Richard ROACH under lease for lives adj Elizabeth REID, Thomas GREGG; and 68a nr south branch of Katockton Creek called "White Oak Bottom" adj Thomas GREGG. All parcels were part of estate of James McILHANY dec'd and alloted to Lewis and Rozannah. Witness: Henry PEERS, M. H. RUST, John H. CANBY, Nich's. PEERS. Certificate of examination for Rosannah returned by Notley C. WILLIAMS, Abiel JENNERS. *Proven 14 April 1812 by John H. CANBY, Nicholas PEERS & Henry PEERS as to ELLZEY & OSBURN.*

Bk:Pg: 01:124 Date: 6 December 1796

Col. Charles ESKRIDGE of Loudoun to Samuel LOVE Esqr. of Loudoun. Bargain and sale of interest in land now in possession of Samuel LOVE and formerly purchased by father of LOVE from ESKRIDGE and also one other tract adjoining previous tract also in possession of LOVE and formerly owned by Richard ESKRIDGE. Witness: J. B. SWANN, Tho. SWANN, Chs. J. LOVE. *Proven 9 January 1797 by Thomas SWANN.*

Bk:Pg: 01:125 Date: 18 August 1791

Charles ESKRIDGE, Gent. of Loudoun and Samuel LOVE, Gent. of Loudoun. Bargain and sale of interest in 2 tracts of land which Carr Wilson LANE & wife Penelope conveyed to LOVE which lands Charles has now by virtue of his intermarriage with Ann mother of Carr of claim of dower. Witness: W. ELLZEY, William ESKRIDGE, W. Wm. LANYAN.

Bk:Pg: 01:126 – 01:127 Date: 3 June 1771

David EVENS/EVANS of Chester Co. Pa to William CARNAN of Loudoun. Lease of 168¾a adj John CRESWELL, John DAVIS, Abraham LAY and Robert CARTER Esqr. Witness: W. Isaac DAVIS, Whitehead WEATHERBY, Joshua EVENS.

Bk:Pg: 01:128 Date: 27 June 1837

Mr. James JENNEY let the bearer Meses [Mrs.] WADE have 50 lbs. of flower or corn meal for the use of the poor deduct 50 cents worth of meal out of the 50 lbs. which she says she owes you. Signed Jess EVANS.

Bk:Pg: 01:129 – 01:130 Date: 9 March 1805

Articles of agreement between William H. HARDING attorney in fact for Ferdinando FAIRFAX of 1st part, Thomas Atwood DIGGES of 2nd part, Joseph LEWIS of 3rd part and Amos JONES Admr with the will annexed of Abel JAN[N]EY dec'd of 4th part. Adjustment of boundaries for land called Piedmont from the will of George William FAIRFAX a purchaser under the original patentee John COLVILL & to the other tract known as Shannondale from the will of George William FAIRFAX the patentee and said DIGGES heir at law to George ATWOOD who desires title from a patent bearing date 26 September 1737 and Joseph LEWIS Junr who purchased of Ferdinando FAIRFAX and said Amos JAN[N]EY deriving title from the will of Abel JAN[N]EY dec'd who's patent was granted to

Catesby COCK on 22 May 1739. Witness: Jno. MATHIAS, Wm. Byrd PAGE, Wm. CHILTON, Fleet SMITH. We the undersigned tenants of Sarah FAIRFAX and purchasees of Joseph LEWIS Jr. agree that the corners this day agreed upon shall be binding. Signed Michael EVERHART, Mathias SMITH, Peter DAIRY, David AXLINE, Adam MILLER. *Proven 9 September 1805 by Wm. B. PAGE. Acknowledged by Jo. LEWIS & W. H. HARDY & John CANBY. Proven 10 September 1805 by J. MATTHIAS & W. CHILTON. Proven 14 October 1805 by Simon SHOVER.*

Bk:Pg: 01:131 – 01:134 Date: 22 September 1805

Nathaniel DAVISSON & wife Nancy of Loudoun to Easter GREGG of Loudoun. Bargain and sale 268a in Harrison Co Va. granted Nathaniel from Commonwealth 25 Jul 1803. Acknowledged by DAVISSON in court 9 December 1805 and ordered certified to Harrison County.

Bk:Pg: 01:135 – 01:136 Date: 11 March 1800

Paulsor DERRY of Loudoun and Michael EVERHARD of Loudoun. Assignment of lease – George William FAIRFAX Esqr. by George NICHOLAS his attorney in fact on 11 June 1787 leased unto DERRY 120a under lease for lives for DERRY and his two sons Jacob and Peter DERRY. Land adj George SHOCKHART, ___ DIGGES, Samuel WALTMAN, John BOOTH. Witness: Wm. H. HARDING, Levi HOLE, John MARTIN Juner. *Proven 8 September 1800 by W. H. HARDING.*

Bk:Pg: 01:137 – 01:138 Date: 7 January 1804

Charles DUNKIN to John JOHNSON. Bill of sale for negro man slave for life Ross now about 34y of age. Witness: Israel LACEY, Wm. COOKE, Nath'l. SKINNER. *Proven 15 May 1804 by Nath'l. SKINNER. Proven 15 May 1804 by Nat'l. SKINNER.*

Bk:Pg: 01:139 Date: 1 November 1805

Henry M. DAVIS of Leesburg to John RIGOR of Leesburg. Bill of sale for negro girl Sall. Witness: William BEATTY, Henry GLASSGOW.

Bk:Pg: 01:140 – 01:141 Date: 10 October 1793

Bates DORSEY to James D'Mauville LANE. Bargain and sale for ¾a at a place called Wappin adj. Francis ADAMS, Newton & John KEENE (which formerly was in possession of David BOYD dec'd) two lotts of Samuel LOVE's in Centerville purchased of George RALLS & Carr Willson LANE & the lands of George RALLS and John Miller CARSON. Witness: Will'm LANYON, Ann LANE. 16 October 1793 received of James D'Mauville LANE £3 the consideration within expressed p me. Signed Betis DORSEY. Witness: Will'm. LANYAN, John VALLANDIGHAM. *Proven 14 April 1794 by Wm. LANE Jr. & cert'd.*

Bk:Pg: 01:142 Date: 29 August 1816

James DONOUGH & wife Kizziah of Leesburg to Francis TRIPLETT Junr. of Leesburg. Bargain and sale of 1a (part of the poorhouse land nr Leesburg sold by commissioners to DONOUGH 6 June 1815) being Lot No. 5 on plat of division of poorhouse land. Witness: John NEWTON, Daniel GRENWALT. 29 August 1816 received of Francis TRIPLETT Junr. $120. 4 November 1816 - Thomas FOUCHE & John McCORMICK Justices of the Peace in Loudoun certify that Kesiagh DONAGH wife of James DONAGH was examined privily and willing signed the above deed.

Bk:Pg: 01:144 – 01:145 Date: 15 March 1806

Mungo DYKES & wife Ann of Leesburg to John McCORMICK of Leesburg. Bargain and sale of 9a Lot No. 4 on Catocton Mt. nr Leesburg laid out by Capt. Robt. BRADEN on land which Jas. HAMILTON formerly held for which he made David LACEY a deed and LACEY conveyed to DYKES. Witness: C. BINNS, Eli OFFUTT, Saml. M. EDWARDS. *Proven 1 November 1830 by Eli OFFUTT.*

Bk:Pg: 01:146 Date: 3 September 1817

Jason DAVIS, brother and principal legatee of Joseph DAVIS dec'd certifies that he gives full consent that the trustees named in a deed of trust given by his dec'd brother to secure a debt owed to Henry DAY for the purchase of 87a on Kittoctin Creek do proceed to sell the land to pay debts. Witness: Towns'd. D. PEYTON, Sarah L. DREAN, Chas. G. ESKRIDGE, Charles DOUGLAS.

Bk:Pg: 01:147 – 01:148 Date: 24 March 1824

Thomas DRAKE of Loudoun of 1st part, Henson ELLIOTT of 2nd part, and John ORR of Loudoun of 3rd part. Trust to ELLIOTT using 53¼a adj Stephen McPHERSON, Thomas CLEWS. Witness: Roger CHEW, John CHAMBLIN, Abner JURY.

Bk:Pg: 01:149 – 01:151 Date: 23 August 1804

Moses DOWDELL of Prince William Co. to Robert ARMISTEAD of Loudoun. Bargain and sale of 112a in Loudoun. Witness: Israel LACEY, G'o. B. WHITING, John H. HARWOOD.

Bk:Pg: 01:152 – 01:153 Date: __ May 1765

Benjamin DAVIS of Loudoun to Andrew SWILLABACK of Loudoun. Assignment of lease (John CARLYLE attorney in fact for George William FAIRFAX Esqr. on 1 May 1761 gave lease for lives to

William HURLEY (his brother Philip HURLEY and his son Stephen HURLEY) transferred on 8 September 1763 to DAVIS) for 100 acres in Loudoun. [no witnesses listed]

Bk:Pg: 01:154 – 01:155 Date: 9 May 1803
Moses DILLON of Loudoun to Burr POWELL Esqr. and Solomon BETTON of Loudoun. Trust for debt to James GARNETT and John T. BROOKE Admrs. of James MERCER Esqr. dec'd using 343½a (part of land of James MERCER dec'd). Witness: Stacy TAYLOR, Francis HEREFORD, W. ELLZEY, Peter DOW.

Bk:Pg: 01:156 Date: 12 April 1816
Amos DONOHOE to David WOODDY (security on note given DONOHOE to William CARR) Trust using household items. Witness: Jesse DAILEY, Henry BENEDUM. *Proven 15 April 1816 by Henry BENEDUM.*

Bk:Pg: 01:157 – 01:158 Date: 29 November 1816
Margaret DIVERS of Loudoun to Samuel DUNKIN of Loudoun. Bargain and sale of interest in 158a (Peter OVERFIELD dec'd left by will to John DIVERS and wife Catharine and at their death divided among their five children, including daughter Margaret). Witness: Wm. DUNKIN, Henry HUTCHISON, Gabriel GREEN, Eli DIVERS, John DIVERS. *Proven 19 Jul 1817 by W. DUNKIN & H. HUTCHISON.*

Bk:Pg: 01:159 – 01:161 Date: 2? [creased] December 1794
John DORSCH & wife Christena of Loudoun to David MARTIN of Loudoun. Bargain and sale of 14½a adj Francis COST, widow WOOLF. Witness: John DAVIS, Levy PRINCE, Frederick STONEBURNER. Proven 14 April 1795 by Jno. DAVIS & Levi PRINCE & ack'd.

Bk:Pg: 01:162 – 01:163 Date: 16 October 1828
John DREAN of Loudoun to Ann M. DREAN of Loudoun and Emily H. STOCKTON (wife of William S. STOCKTON formerly Emily H. DREAN) of Philadelphia PA. Gift of lot on south side of Market St. in Leesburg with dwelling house and the school room, adj lot he recently gave to daughter Sarah SEEDERS (deed dated 1 October 1828), lot of late Sampson BLINCOE. Subject to an annuity of $50/annum for six years to be paid to his daughter Eliza RALPH wife of Edward RALPH. Witness: Thos. MORALLEE, Francis S. BOGUE, Josiah L. DREAN. *Proven 2 April 1829 by Josiah DREAN & Francis BOGUE.*

Bk:Pg: 01:164 – 01:167 Date: 8 November 1814
William Dudley DIGGS & wife Ellanorah of Prince George Co. Md to Catharine NEISWANGER of Loudoun. Bargain and sale of 1a now in possession of Catharine adj DIGGES, ___ DEMERY, ___ NEISWANGER. Witness: Theodore SHEKLES, William Brent CARROLL, John S. POWER. Proven by Thomas BOWIE and Geo. PAGE in Prince George Co. 8 November 1814. Certificate of examination on 8 November 1814 for Ellanorah DIGGES returned by Thomas BOWIE and George PAGE, Gent. of Prince George Co. Md. *Proven 8 May 1815 by Theodore SHECKLES & Wm. B. CARROLL.*

Bk:Pg: 01:168 and 01:170 Date: 10 April 1784
John DREAN, couper, & wife Nancy, of Leesburg to George HAMMETT cordwaner of Leesburg. Bargain and sale of 600 sq ft. Lot No. __ in Leesburg adj Andrew SPICHTS, Back St. (part of lot conveyed by Daniel LOSH & wife to DREAN 15 September 1779). Witness: Charles BINNS Jr., Osborn KING, Samuel HOUGH.

Bk:Pg: 01:169 Date: __ April 1814
John DAVIS of Leesburg. Deed of manumission for one negro woman slave Amey now in his possession when she arrives at age of 35y, she being born on 4 May 1791, will be free on 4 May 1826. Manumits one negro boy slave Aquila when he arrives at age of 25y which will be on 20 August 1827. Manumits negro boy slave George when he arrives at age of 25y, which will be on 20 October 1835. Manumits negro girl slave Alsinda when she arrives at age of 21y, which will be on 21 May 1833. Provided male offspring of above women shall serve him till they arrive at age of 25y, when they will be manumitted. Female offspring of above women shall serve him until they arrive at age of 21y. Witness: Thomas SANDERS, Daniel McALISTER. *Proven 14 December 1814 by Thomas SANDERS.*

Bk:Pg: 01:170 – 01:171 Date: 10 April 1784
John DREAN of Loudoun to George HAMMETT of Loudoun. Bargain and sale of 600 sq. foot lot in Leesburg (conveyed to John DREAN by Daniel LOSH & wife 1779). Witness: Charles BINNS Jr., Osborn KING, Samuel HOUGH. *Proven 9 August 1784 by Chas. BINNS Jr. & affirm'd of Saml. HOUGH.*

Bk:Pg: 01:172 – 01:175 Date: 1 January 1791
Benjamin DULANY of Fairfax to Robert POWELL (and wife Elizabeth) of Loudoun. Lease for lives of 133½a adj land on which ___ WELSH a tenant of DULANY's lived, land on which ___ MIDDLETON a tenant of DULANY's lived, Malachi CUMMINS, ___ HUFF also a tenant. Witness: James LEWIS, John MIDDLETON,

Benj'n. Jas. DULANY. 14 September 1791 – Robert POWELL assigns over all interest of within lease to Robert FULTON. Witness: Rt. BRADEN Jr., David FULTON, Robert FULTON Junr. *Proven 9 April 1792 by Js. LEWIS & John MIDDLETON & cert'd.*

Bk:Pg: 01:176 – 01:178 Date: 23 February 1807
Thomas DORRELL of Loudoun to Thomas GREGG of Loudoun. Bill of sale for household items, farm animals, crops, etc. Witness: James H. HAMILTON, James COPELAND, Thomas LOVE. *Proven 14 September 1807 by Jas. COPELAND & Thomas LOVE & o. cert'd.*

Bk:Pg: 01:179 – 01:181 Date: 13 November 1813
John DODD Junr. of Loudoun to John DRISH of Loudoun. Bargain and sale of 60 sq perch lot in Leesburg (purchased of Presley SAUNDERS Jr. & wife Mary 16 March 1811) adj Thomas JACOBS' purchase of __ SUTHERLAND, ___ SAUNDERS' purchased of ___ NIXON, ___ WRIGHT's purchase of SAUNDERS. Witness: Thos. R. MOTT, E. OFFUTT, Thomas P. KNOX. *Proven 12 January 1814 by E. OFFUTT & Tho. R. MOTT.*

Bk:Pg: 01:182 Date: 11 April 1795
William DULIN of Cameron Parish in Loudoun to sons Lewis DULIN and Gerrard DULIN equally. Bill of sale for one negro girl Sall now in possession of Marmaduke Bro'y BECKWITH (leased for the present year) and household items. Witness: Anthony ETHELL, Joseph ASBURY. *Proven 1799 by Anthony ETHELL.*

Bk:Pg: 01:183 Date: 11 August 1809
John DEMERY of Loudoun to John CONNARD of Loudoun. Bill of sale for negro woman Jane. Witness: Nicholas ROPP, Philip DERRY, Caleb NEEDHAM. *Proven 11 September 1809 by Philip DERRY.*

Bk:Pg: 01:184 Date: 10 December 1800
Deed of examination for Parnella DAVIS wife of David DAVIS for sale of 100a to William ELLZEY. Returned by A. RUSSEL, Richard COLEMAN.

Bk:Pg: 01:185 – 01:186 Date: 1 April 1797
Richard DAVISS to John SPENCER. Bargain and sale of 100a formerly called John DAVISS's lot adj plantation of John SPENCER purchased of John PILES at Broad Run Church and including the store house DAVISS is now erecting, and also including two tracts of land one containing (by surveys of 21 June 1784) 922a on Coburns Creek and waters of Buthes Creek

and other tract of 922a on Colvins Creek and Buthes Creek which William HEPBURN sold to David DAVIS and David to Richard DAVISS. Witness: William HARRISON, Josiah VANSKIVER, Moses SPENCER, William SPENCER.

This deed being given as security to secure John SPENCER from expense & cost that might be hath for in being security for Amos DAVISS for £100 and costs arising from the same. Signed John SPENCER. Witness: Wm. HARRISON, Josiah VANSKIVER, William SPENCER. Proven 9 October 1797 by Josiah VANSKIVER & Wm. SPENCER.

Bk:Pg: 01:187 Date: 5 January 1796

John DICKS of Loudoun to Isaac VANDEVANDER of Loudoun. Bargain and sale of 10a with dwelling house adj Obed PIERPOINT, Charles BENNETT (part of tract now in possession of VANDEVANDER). Witness: John DODD, Farling BALL Junr., R. BRADEN. *Proven 11 Jul 1796 by John DODD.*

Bk:Pg: 01:188 – 01:190 Date: 8 August 1796

Brawner DOWDLE of Fauquier to Moses DOWDLE of Loudoun. Bargain and sale of __a in Loudoun nr Bull Run Mt. in Cameron Parish which was bequeathed to George DOWDLE dec'd father of Brawner and Moses by Thomas DOWDLE dec'd father of George by will recorded in Fairfax. Tract adj Joseph HUTCHISON, Thomas FLOOD now ARMSTEAD. Witness: P. BAYLY, W. P. BAYLY, Israel LACEY, Jno. BAYLY, Avary DOWDELL. Memorandum: agreed between Brawner and Moses that Elinor DOWDLE their mother who now lived on the land shall not be disturbed but shall have a wright {sic} to live on land during her life. *Proven 13 March 1797 by W. P. BAYLEY & J. LACY.*

Bk:Pg: 01:191 – 01:192 Date: 7 April 1803

Benjamin DEWELL of Loudoun to Thomas Ludwell LEE and Landon CARTER Esquires Exors. of George CARTER dec'd. Trust using 107a on south side of Secolon Branch purchased of LEE and CARTER this day. Witness: Jno. MATHIAS, Samuel DONOHOE, Obadiah CLIFFORD, Thos. FOUCH. *Proven 10 April 1803 by John MATHIAS & Obadiah CLIFFORD.*

Bk:Pg: 01:193 – 01:194 Date: 7 February 1808

Nancy DAVISSON of Loudoun to John WHITE of Loudoun. Bargain and sale of a tenement or lot formerly in occupation of Esther GREGG dec'd by virtue of a lease granted by John TAYLOE Esqr. dec'd or his agent to a James TOBIN dec'd. Except the dower of Margaret McILHANY widow of James McILHANY dec'd from whom tenement descended to Nancy. Witness: Lewis ELLZEY, William WHITE, Tho. WHITE.

Bk:Pg: 01:195 – 01:196 Date: 2 January 1802

To Jos. LANE, William H. POWELL & Benj'n. GRAYSON, Gentlemen. Requests they exam Uree DRAKE wife of Thomas DRAKE for deed of 11 January 1802 on 100a to Isaac RICHARDS (see below). Returned 11 January 1802 by Wm. H. POWELL, Ben. GRAYSON.

Bk:Pg: 01:197 – 01:198 Date: 11 January 1802

Thomas DRAKE & wife Uree to Isaac RICHARDS of Loudoun. Bargain and sale of 100a adj Benjamin BARTON. Witness: Benjamin BARTON, Ben. GRAYSON, Abner HUMPHREY, Wm. H. POWELL, Jos. LEWIS, Junr. *Proven 11 January 1802 by Benjamin BARTON & Abner HUMPHREY.*

Bk:Pg: 01:199 – 01:200 Date: 8 April 1776

Benjamin DOWNS of Loudoun to Henry DOWNS of Loudoun. Assignment of lease of 150a (leased from Bryant FAIRFAX of Fairfax to Benjamin on 21 September 1767). Witness: Leven POWELL, James BATTSON, Benjamin CLARK. *Proven 13 May 1776 by Leven POWELL & James BATTSON.*

Bk:Pg: 01:201 – 01:202 Date: 21 January 1797

Charles DUNKIN & wife Susannah of Loudoun to Matthew HARRISON Junr. now of Loudoun. Bargain and sale of 95¾a (part of Charter's tract where he now lives) adj ___ TURLEY, Piney branch, ___ FOSTER. Witness: Nancy DUNCAN, Wm. H. HARDING, Catharine DUNCAN, Susanna DUNCAN.

Bk:Pg: 01:203 – 01:204 Date: 28 March 1800

David DAVIES of Loudoun to William ELLZEY of Loudoun. Bargain and sale of 200a on Goose Creek (land leased by Kitchen PRIMM to Lewis STOLE lease executed 11 October 1768). Witness: Absalom HAWLEY, Alex'r. MILTON, A. RUSSEL. *Proven 14 September 1800 by Alex. MELTON & A. HALLEY.*

Bk:Pg: 01:205 – 01:207 Date: 19 January 1805

James DAWSON of Leesburg to Jonas POTTS & Obadiah CLIFFORD of Leesburg. Trust using a brick house and part of Lot No. 5 where DAWSON now lives on Loudoun St. adj John SHAW, Patrick CAVAN dec'd. Witness: John CAVAN, Thos. JACOBS, William DULIN. *Proven 11 September 1805 by Thos. JACOBS & John CAVAN.*

Bk:Pg: 01:208 – 01:211 Date: 12 April 1797

Thomas DAVIS & wife Leah of Loudoun to John A. BINNS of Loudoun. Bargain and sale of 139¾a conveyed to DAVIS from Henry Astley BENNETT Esqr (except 5a which DAVIS conveyed to Isaac BALL). Witness: C. BINNS Jr., Alexander SUTHERLAND, Philip TRIPLETT. Certificate of examination for Leah returned by John LITTLETON, Samuel MURREY dated 24 May 1797. *Proven 11 September 1797 by Charles BINNS & Alexander SUTHERLAND.*

Bk:Pg: 01:212 Date: 2 May 1818

Clerk is requested to deliver to Mr. Saml. DANIEL a mortgage or deed of trust lodged in his care & proven or partially proven on 1,500a of Ohio land given to secure the payment of some money coming on the purchase of that land to the estate of Col. L. POWELL dec'd. Signed Burr POWELL acting Exor. of L. P. dec'd.

Bk:Pg: 01:213 Date: 7 July 1838

James B. DODD of Loudoun to S. B. T. CALDWELL of Loudoun. Trust to secure sundry notes using interest in negro girl Maria. [no witness signatures]

Bk:Pg: 01:214 – 01:215 Date: 10 July 1848

Amos DENHAM to William BELL Sheriff of Fauquier Co. DENHAM now in jail in Loudoun on 5 executions (one in name of James H. BITZER ass'ee of Joshua TAYLOR, one in name of Jesse RICHARDS, one in name of William McPHERSON, one in name of Henry W. HOPE, one in name of Stephen REED) being for the use of John L. GILL. Conveys 35a (deed by DENHAM to John C. MURRY for benefit of Caleb RECTOR, Andrew BELMARE & C. T. DENHAM recorded in Fauquier) per act of relief of the Insolvent Debtor. Acknowledged by DENHAM 10 July 1848 before F. W. LUCKETT, C. C. McINTYRE.

Bk:Pg: 01:216 Date: 2 September 1833

George DONOHOE, Edward TILLETT, and Jos. E. STONESTREET distributees of James TILLETT dec'd admit that each has been advanced by Hannah TILLETT the Admx about $100 and agree to waive a settlement of the Administration account and to exempt the securities of the Admx from all liability on her account. Witness: Rich. H. HENDERSON, Lewis J. DONOHOE, Francis DONOHOE.

Bk:Pg: 01:217 – 01:223 Date: 16 June 1806

Timothy WHELAN late of Loudoun, storekeeper lately dec'd, devised by his will ½ of his property and effects to his brother James WHELAN and the other ½ to his four sisters then residing in Ireland, namely Margaret WHELAN, Catharine WHELAN, Winnefried

WHELAN and Judith WHELAN. James WHELAN died shortly after Timothy died without possessing any part of the fortune or effects so devised to him by Timothy. By the death of James and Timothy the said Margaret WHELAN otherwise DUNN widow, and Winnefried WHELAN others PHELAN are now each entitled to ¼th of all property of their brothers. Margaret WHELAN otherwise DUNN widow now residing in Darrow in county of Kilkenny in Ireland and Winnefried WHELAN otherwise PHELAN now wife of Jeremiagh PHELAN residing at Ballyguhin in Queens Co. Ireland appoint Edward PHELAN of Abbyleix in Queens Co., Gent. as their lawful attorney. To recover from Maurice DELANY acting Exor. of Timothy WHELAN their share. Also to recover from Terence FIGH their share of estates of brothers. Witness: Edw'd. PHELAN, Thom's. REVINGTON. Proven by REVINGTON in Dublin. *Recorded in Deed Book 2H, page 7.*

Bk:Pg: 01:224 - 01:236 Date: 28 October 1806

Maurice DELANY (sole Exor of Timothy WHELAN) at present residing in Baltimore MD to Edward PHELAN late of Abbyleix in Queens Co. Ireland but now residing in Baltimore. Per above deed regarding disposition of estate based on will of Timothy with James dying intestate. Margaret (still surviving) intermarried with ___ DUNN now deceased, Winnefried intermarried Jeremiagh PHELAN. Considerable debt now owing to estate of Timothy. DELANY transfers to Edw'd. PHELAN part of estate. Witness: John SCOTT. *This PA is recorded in Deed Book 2G, page 514.*

Bk:Pg: 01:237 – 01:238 Date: 28 May 1814

Overseers of the Poor of Loudoun to Joseph BEARD of Loudoun. By Court order of 15 May 1810 Overseers placed John DOBBINS an orphan aged 20y on 1 June 1814 to be an apprentice with BEARD until he is 21y of age, to be taught the trade of a cabinet maker and pay DOBBINS $12 at expiration of term. Signed by Presley CORDELL, Aaron SANDERS, Thos. PHILLIPS, Joseph BEARD. Witness: John HAMMERLY, Alexander CORDELL.

Bk:Pg: 01:239 – 01:240 Date: 29 June 1801

George ROWAN, Asa MOORE and John ROSE Overseers of the Poor for Shelburn Parish to John DRISH of Leesburg. By Court order of 11 May 1801 Overseers bind Asaph DAVIS aged 16y the 7th of March last until he attains the age of 21 years, to be taught the trade of a joiner.

Bk:Pg: 01:241 – 01:244 Date: 1 January 1798

Benjamin DULANY of Fairfax to John MIDDLETON & wife at this time Mary MIDDLETON. Lease for lives of 202a, reserving 50a of woodland for the purpose of rail & board timber. MIDDLETONs agree to plant an orchard, build a dwelling house, pay the taxes, etc. Witness: Robert M. POWELL, W. POWELL, D. DULANY. *Proven 14 May 1798 by Robert POWELL & W. POWELL.*

Bk:Pg: 01:245 – 01:246 Date: 9 April 1810

John DOSHTIMER, Charles DOSHTIMER, Daniel MAY and John YONKIN/YOUNKIN to John S. MARLOW of Loudoun. Bargain and sale of undivided shares of 103½a which Jacob DOSHTIMER dec'd formerly of Loudoun died possessed in Loudoun. Parties of 1st part are entitled to 1/7th part each. Adam SHOVER granted Power of Attorney to convey the interests. Witness: Will'm. MILLS, Jacob FAWLY, Catharine DORFF.

Bk:Pg: 01:247 Date: ___

Robert DICK of Prince George Co. Md factor for Mess'rs. David DALYELL, George OSWALD & Co. Merchants in Glasgow appoint William GRAYSON Attorney at Law of Prince William Co. Va to recover money due from Mess'rs. Fleming PATTERSON and John PATTERSON, Merch'ts. in Leesburg (two bonds dated 11 August 1764). Witness: Wm. RAMSAY, Benj. SEBASTIAN.

Bk:Pg: 01:248 – 01:249 Date: 27 March 1772

Charles DAVIS of Loudoun to Simon TRIPLETT of Loudoun. Bargain and sale of lease for lives on land belonging to estate of William Carr LANE dec'd. Witness: John ORR, Reuben TRIPLETT. 24 August 1772 proven by 2 witnesses.

Bk:Pg: 01:250 Date: 15 June 1810

Commissioners appointed to sell the estate of Obed HARRIS dec'd return a bond of $1,000 signed by James LEGG & Henry WASHINGTON payable in 9 months from 16 March 1810 to Burr POWELL & John SINCLAIR Commissioners.

Bk:Pg: 01:251 Date: 25 December 1810

Return of bond for sale of O. HARRIS estate. Mess'rs. James LEGG & Henry WASHINGTON will please read the within mentioned bond which is filed in Court to me by the bearer Mr. Wm. McCARTY. Unless payment is made April will be ordered agreeably to the directions of the Court. Signed Burr POWELL.

Bk:Pg: 01:252 Date: 10 December 1810

Ordered that the commissioners appointed to sell the estate of Obed HARRIS dec'd do collect the money arising from the sale by suit or otherwise and bring the money into Court subject to the future order. Signed C. BINNS, Ck Cl.

Bk:Pg: 01:253 Date: 15 June 1784
John HOUGH Jr. and John BINNS to Bernard HOUGH. Bond to stay a judgment obtained against John HOUGH Jr. to cover the costs.

Bk:Pg: 01:254 – 01:256 Date: 15 August 1827
Samuel HAMMATT of Loudoun to Joseph T. NEWTON. Trust using 12a Lot No. 7 on Leesburg Turnpike being part of lands of the late Richetts & Newton sold by decree of Circuit Court of Alexandria Co. and 10a Lot No. 9. Witness: Jas. L. MARTIN, James THOMAS, James GILMORE.

Bk:Pg: 01:257 – 01:258 Date: 17 October 1825
William HERBERT Admr. with the will annexed of Ferdinando FAIRFAX of Fairfax Co. to Thomas KIDWELL of Loudoun. Release of mortgage of 2 September 1819 on 50a in Loudoun on side of Blue Ridge Mt. adj. Conrod NEER's heirs, William CLENDENNING. KIDWELL sold 10a adj ___ PURCELL to George KOONCE of Loudoun who paid HERBERT. Witness: Nelson CHAMBLIN, John SHRIVER, Jacob EKMAN, James McBRIDE. *Proven 19 November 1825 by Nelson CHAMBLIN & Jacob ECKMAN.*

Bk:Pg: 01:259 – 01:260 Date: 7 November 1825
William HERBERT Admr. with the will annexed of Ferdinando FAIRFAX of Fairfax Co. to Thomas KIDWELL of Loudoun. Release of mortgage of 2 September 1819 on 50a in Loudoun on side of Blue Ridge Mt. adj Conrod NEER's heirs, William CLENDENNING. KIDWELL sold 5a to Henry SAGLE. Signed William HERBERT by his atty in fact William HICKMAN. Witness: John SHRIVER, Jesse NEER, Joseph NEER, Joshua ROBERTS, George KOONCE. *Proven 14 November 1825 by John SH[R]IVERS.*

Bk:Pg: 01:261 – 01:264 Date: 1 August 1818
William H. HARDEY & wife Elenor of Loudoun of 1st part, Samuel M. EDWARDS of Leesburg of 2nd part and John ROSE & Richard H. HENDERSON of Leesburg of 3rd part. Trust for debt to ROSE and HENDERSON (due by judgment of Superior Court) using 147¼a conveyed to HANDEY by James MOUNT & wife Hannah 25 April 1818, adj. Points OWSLEY, COCKE's Patent. Witness: Thomas A. MOORE, James T. HOPE, E. H. HANDEY. Proven 1 January 1820 by Thos. A. MOORE as to HANDY. *Proven 1 January 1820 by Thomas A. MOORE and William & Eleanor HANDY.*

Bk:Pg: 01:265 – 01:266 Date: 3 September 1813
Isaac HOUGH of Loudoun to Isaac BALL of Loudoun. Bargain and sale of 1a (purchased of Robert BRADEN trustee of Isaac BALL) adj

___ DAVIS, ___ SHAVER. Witness: Jacob BAUGH, John WILLIAMS, John WORSLEY. *Proven 8 November 1813 by Jacob BAUGH & John WORSLEY.*

Bk:Pg: 01:267 – 01:270 Date: 25 Jul 1804

Jemimah HOLLINGSWORTH widow of John HOLLINGSWORTH dec'd and Robert BRADEN and James HEATON trustees to Jonas POTTS. Bargain and sale of 123a on east side of Kittockton Creek adj Catesby COCK (100a and 23a which Rich'd ROACH purchased of E[d]mund SANDS) and 45a (purchased by Richard ROACH of Abraham DAWSON) nr Bald Hill adj Richard WILLIAMS. John HOLLINGSWORTH dec'd in his lifetime by trust dated 10 May 1802 (Deed Book 2B, page 252) conveyed to Robert BRADEN and James HEATON. Defaulted on the payments so tract was sold at public auction on 25 Mar ___. Witness: John STOUSEBERGER, Anthony CONRAD, William JINKINS, Geo. TAVENDER, William GREGG, James ROACH. 10 September 1804 ack'd by Rt. BRADEN and proven as to James HEATON by Anth'y CONNARD, 11th ack'd by James HEATON.

Bk:Pg: 01:271 – 01:273 Date: 8 May 1814

Samuel HOUGH & wife Ann of Loudoun to John POTTER of Loudoun. Bargain and sale of lot in Leesburg. William MANN and Charles F. MERCER commissioners of the Court in suit of Exors. of Daniel MILDRED dec'd surviving partner of MILDRED and ROBERTS against Saml. HOUGH and others sold lot on north side of Loudoun Street in Leesburg adj Thomas SAUNDERS, William TAYLOR to Henry CLAGETT of Leesburg, deed dated 14 November 1807. CLAGETT & wife Julia sold part of lot to John POTTER. Ann wife of Samuel HOUGH never relinquished her dower and now wishes to do so. Witness: Geo. W. BALL, William CARR, Saml. CLAPHAM. Certificate of examination of Ann returned 3 May 1814 by Saml. CLAPHAM and William CARR. *Proven 14 June 1814 by George BALL & William CARR.*

Bk:Pg: 01:274 – 01: 276 Date: 18 January 1810

William HOUGH of Loudoun to James MOORE & John WILLIAMS of Loudoun. Bargain and sale of 4,800 sq ft lot in Waterford adj Flemon PATTESON. Witness: Thomas PHILLIPS, Daniel STONE, Asa MOORE. *Proven 11 January 1810 by Daniel STONE & Thomas PHILLIPS.*

Bk:Pg: 01:277 Date: 14 May 1796

Elizabeth HANCOCK to Lewis ELLZEY. Bargain and sale of tract on broad run bequeath to LEWIS per will of his father William ELLZEY.

Witness: A. RUSSEL, Saml. ADAMS, Michel SCHRYOCK. *Proven 13 February 1797 by A. RUSSELL & M. SCHRYOCK.*

Bk:Pg: 01:278 – 01:279 Date: 3 September 1813
Isaac HOUGH of Loudoun to Daniel DAVIS of Loudoun. Bargain and sale of 1a on Broad Run adj Isaac BALL, ___ SHAVER. Witness: Abiel JENNERS, Jacob BAUGH, John SHAVER, John WILLIAMS. [see page 01:282] *Proven 8 November 1813 by Jacob BAUGH.*

Bk:Pg: 01:280 – 01:281 Date: __ April 1804
Mahlon HOUGH of Loudoun to Nancy GREGORY of Loudoun. Bargain and sale of ¼a on Kitoctin Creek adj. Col. TAYLOE, Thos. LESLEY. Witness: Edward CANARD Junr., Josiah POTTS, Robert R. HOUGH, Mahlon MORRIS. *Proven 10 September 1804 by Edward CONNARD & proven 22 August 1838 by Mahlon MORRIS.*

Bk:Pg: 01:282 Date: 3 September 1813
Certificate of examination for Fanny HOUGH wife of Isaac HOUGH for bargain and sale of 28 August 1813 to John SHAVER of 10a. Returned by Abiel JENNERS, R. BRADEN. [*This should go with Deed beginning on p. 283*]

Bk:Pg: 01:283 – 01:286 Date: 28 August 1813
Isaac HOUGH & wife Fanny of Loudoun to John SHAVER of Loudoun. Bargain and sale of 10a of land as described here. Trust by Isaac BALL dated 28 August 1805 conveyed to James HAMILTON and Robert BRADEN 5a on Broad run adj lot formerly James FERGUSON's (now Isaac BALL's) and lot at Ball mill tail now laid off by Stephen and John BALL so as to include 9a of the lott of land which Farling BALL dec'd bought of HOOE and LITTLE and sold to Isaac. James HAMILTON died and BRADEN sold land agreeable to trust. Witness: Jacob BAUGH, John WILLIAMS, John WORSLEY. Proven 8 November 1813 by Jacob BAUGH & Jno. WORSLEY & o. certified. *Proven 8 November 1813 by Jacob BAUGH & John WORSLEY. See page 282.*

Bk:Pg: 01:287 – 01:288 Date: 30 September 1826
William HAGERMAN & wife Elizabeth of Loudoun to Lewis BERKELEY of Loudoun. Bargain and sale of Lot No. 50 in Aldie. Witness: Thos. ROBINSON, ??? [paper torn], William S. ADAMS. *Proven 13 October 1825 by Thomas ROBINSON.*

Bk:Pg: 01:289 Date: 29 August 1833
Mary D. HALLEY of Loudoun to John L. WILSON of Loudoun. Bargain and sale of 190a on Elk Lick adj Jeremiah & Hampton

HALLEY, Andrew HEATH. Witness: Jas. MERSHON, L. F. MANKIN, Wm. SAFFER. *Proven 21 May 1835 by James MERSHON.*

Bk:Pg: 01:290 Date: 25 March 1833

Articles of agreement between William T. HOUGH of Loudoun and John WOOLFORD and William VIRTS Junr. of Loudoun. Bargain and sale of land where HOUGH now lives – agreement on payments. Witness: William MOORE, John WHITE, Thos. J. MARLOW.

Bk:Pg: 01:291 – 01:292 Date: 10 August 1833

Samuel HAMMONTREE of Loudoun to Ariss BUCKNER Sheriff of Loudoun. HAMMONTREE delivered to Sheriff by George TURNER his special bail in suit of Wm. C. PALMER, surrenders house and lot in Union adj John ANDERSON, Mahlon BALDWIN to secure costs. [no witness signatures]

Bk:Pg: 01:293 – 01:295 Date: 1 April 1846

Mary T. HOUGH, Eleanor C. HOUGH, Thomas HOUGH & wife Hannah, William HOUGH & wife Louesia L. and Joseph S. HOUGH & wife Mary W. to Hiram McVEIGH, all of Loudoun. Bargain and sale of 1/16th acre nr Hillsburgh on Catoctin Creek, LESLIE's lot, road to Ramsberg & Cover's Factory. Acknowledged 16 January 1847.

Bk:Pg: 01:296 – 01:297 Date: 16 October 1830

Saml. HIXSON of Loudoun to Elizabeth COPELAND of Loudoun. Gift of household items. Witness: A. S. ANDERSON, S. HOUGH, J. T. GRIFFITH, George GREGG.

Bk:Pg: 01:298 – 01:299 Date: 21 December 1799

James HIXSON of Northumberland Co. Pa to William PAXSON of Loudoun. Bargain and sale of undivided interest to his father William HIXSON's landed estate which said share is 27a. Timothy PAXSON Senior, David HIXSON, Wm. WALLACE Junr. Proven 11 August 1800 by Tim'o. HIXSON Sr. *Proven 11 August 1800 by David HIXSON.*

Bk:Pg: 01:300 – 01:301 Date: 14 June 1806

Daniel HIXSON of Ross Co. Northwest Territory bound to William PAXSON of Loudoun. HIXSON sold to PAXSON his undivided right of the plantation on which his father formerly lived containing 220a (1/8th part thereof being 28a). Agreement on payment and deed. Witness: David HIXSON, William MAINS, Timothy HIXSON. *Proven 9 September 1806 by David HIXSON & William MAINS.*

Bk:Pg: 01:302 – 01:303 Date: 21 December 1799
Timothy HIXSON Junior & wife Sarah of Loudoun to William PAXTON/PAXSON of Loudoun. Bargain and sale of 27a. Witness: Timothy HIXSON Senior, Wm. WALLACE Junr., David HIXSON. 11 August 1800 proven by Tim'o. HIXSON Senr.

Bk:Pg: 01:304 Date: 30 March 1813
Certificate of examination for Susannah DRISH wife of Charles DRISH for bargain and sale of 75a to William NEWTON. Returned by Wm. B. HARRISON, Samuel MURREY.

Bk:Pg: 01:305 Date: ___ 1762
John GLADIN & wife Mary by lease/release dated 7 & 8 February 1762 to Robert ADAM sold ½a in Leesburg, parish of Cameron. Request for certificate of examination of Mary.

Bk:Pg: 01:306 Date: 19 June 1811
Sale has been made by commissioners appointed by court to sell the slaves belonging to estate of Obed HARRIS dec'd for distribution among the heirs. James LEGG became the purchaser and gave bond with Henry WASHINGTON Esqr. as security which is now due. Request by Elezebeth HARRIS to fix the sum that she is entitled to. Witness: A. GIBSON. Jas. LEGG & Hy. WASHINGTON vs B. POWELL & J. SINCLAIR Commrs. app'd by Court to make sale of the estate and slaves of Obed HARRIS dec'd for penalty of $1,000 conditioned for pay't. of $500 nine months from date of bond, dated 16th March 1810. Delivered to Burr POWELL one of the Commrs. agreeable to an order of the Court. Signed S. M. EDWARDS, 12 March 1811

Bk:Pg: 01:307 Date: 25 April 1788 in Montgomery Co Md
Certifies that Samuel HOUGH has the consent of a free negro woman Affee to take her child Rose BROOKE, 4 years old on the 1st day of May last, into Loudoun and she also consents that you bind Rose to said HOUGH provided that Rose be taught to read and write the English language and when free will also furnish her with a suit of decent cloath. Signed Basil BROOKE.

Bk:Pg: 01:308 – 01:310 Date: 12 April 1802
Adam HOUSHOLDER Junr. of Loudoun to John HALL of Jefferson Co. Va. Assignment of unexpired lease. George William FAIRFAX Esqr. granted lease to George WRIGHT for 60a, WRIGHT assigned lease to Farling BALL, Farling by trust empowered John LITTLEJOHN & James POTTS to sell to pay debts but afterwards assigned to his son Isaac BALL and Isaac by trust empowered same trustees to sell to pay debts. LITTLEJOHN & POTTS sold residue of

unexpired term by trust to John JANNEY Senr. since dec'd and Adam HOUSHOLDER Junr. Witness: Isaac LAROWE. Ack'd by HOUSHOLDER 13 April 1802. Assignment of lease - Receipt dated 3 January 1810 by John HALL assigning lease to John BALL who paid $1,000. Witness: R. BRADEN, John WILLIAMS, John HAMILTON, Isaac HOUGH, Jonas POTTS. *Proven 8 January 1810 by Robert BRADEN & Jonas POTTS.*

Bk:Pg: 01:311 Date: 24 April 1779

Isaac HUMPHREY of Loudoun to Thomas HUMPHREY of Loudoun. Lease of 227a adj Hanah BROOKS, Leven POWELL. Witness: Thomas DRAKE, Samuel BUTCHER, Benj'n. BARTON.

Bk:Pg: 01:312 - 01:314 Date: 7 March 1810

Joseph HAINES & wife Maria late Maria HANDEY of Loudoun to William H. HANDEY of Loudoun. Assignment of share of real & personal estate from inventory as also land and mills on Goose Creek (deed by Rawleigh COLSTON & wife Elizabeth for the same) to Given HANDEY and the children, heirs & legal reps of John HANDEY dec'd bearing date 21 September 1807. Maria is entitled to a full portion of property as one of the children of John dec'd. Witness: Peter TOWPERMAN, John WILSON, Reuben TRAHAM. Certificate of examination for Maria returned 10 March 1810 by Wm. BRONAUGH, Step. C. ROSZEL. *Proven 14 May 1810 by Peter TOWPERMAN & John WILSON.*

Bk:Pg: 01:315 Date: ___

Deed & Comr. – M. HOUGH & wife to P. HUFFMAN, May Ct. 1807 ord'd. to be certif'd. to the D. of Columbia. Certif'd. accordingly & delivered to Robert J. TAYLOR atty. for HUFFMAN at Nov. Ct. 1808. Signed Saml. M. EDWARDS.

Bk:Pg: 01:316 – 01:319 Date: 14 December 1792

Josiah HERBERT of Loudoun to George THOMPSON of Loudoun. Bargain and sale of lease of 100a. Thomas Ludwell LEE Esqr. granted lease for lives on 21 December 1773 to Jacob MORRISS (wife Elizabeth and Charles DAWSON the 5th son of John DAWSON). Witness: Thomas HERBERT, Isaac TOBIN, Nathanel TOBIN. 13 May 1793 proven by Ths. HUMPHREY [HERBERT?] & I. TOBIN & cert'd. *Proven 13 May 1793 by Thomas HUMPHREY.* [HERBERT?]

Bk:Pg: 01:320 – 01:321 Date: 24 April 1781

Palser HESS, blacksmith of Loudoun to John GILES of Loudoun. Assignment of lease on 150a on north side of Broad Run. Henry ASHTON late of Westmoreland Co. on 11 December 1754 granted lease for lives to William HANCOCKE (and sons Simon & William HANCOCKE) on two 150a adjoining lots both on Broad run of Potomack in Loudoun. HANCOCKE assigned lease to Daniel NEALE, and NEALE to Robert SANDFORD. Witness: John MINOR, Elias COCKERIL, Thomas MINOR, Daniel JENINGS. *Proven 14 May 1781 by John MINOR & Danl. JENNINGS & cert.*

Bk:Pg: 01:322 – 01:323 Date: 23 November 1811

John HAMMERLY & wife Jane of Loudoun to Francis PEYTON of Loudoun. Mortgage on part of lot in Leesburg which John DRISH purchased of Henry McCABE, adj DRISH, ___ MIDDLETON, ___ CORDEL. Witness: Sam. M. EDWARDS. 14 January 1812 ackn'd & o. r'd. Recorded Liber 6-O folio 219. [should be 2O:219] Release of mortgage proven 23 November 1819 by L. W. DENHAM & A. O. POWEL.

Bk:Pg: 01:324 – 01:327 Date: 24 December 1811

Nathaniel HOVEY of borough of Harrisburg, Dauphin Co. Pa of 1st part, James CURTIS of Loudoun of 2nd part and Ths. WILKINSON of Loudoun of 3rd part. Trust for debt to WILKINSON using 440a in Armstrong township, Indiana Co. late Westmoreland Co. Pa conveyed to HOVEY by John CAROTHERS 6 December 1811 which was warranted to Henry BUCK and conveyed by Alexander JOHNSTON Esqr. Sheriff of Westmoreland Co. on 21 Jul 1808 to Samuel GUTHRIE Esqr. and by GUTHRIE to Daniel STANDARD, then to John CAROTHERS. Witness: Rich'd. H. HENDERSON, Saml. M. EDWARDS, Eli OFFUTT. 12 March 1812 p'd by witness as to H. & C. & o. c.

Bk:Pg: 01:328 Date: 20 November 1807

Jesse HARRISS & wife Margaret to son George HARRISS of Fairfield Co. Ohio. Power of attorney to receive money from sale of lands that Augustine LOVE was authorized to sell from the Exors. of George HIXSON dec'd. LOVE is discharged. Witness: Silas REES, William LANHAM. *Proven 9 May 1808 by Silas REES.*

Bk:Pg: 01:329 Date: 27 February 1807

Memorandum of an agreement between George HAMMAT of Loudoun and James WINTERS of Loudoun. HAMMAT leased to WINTERS a lot whereon WINTERS now lives for the present year to end 17 Oct next for 1/3 part of the corn & fodder, oats, flax, potatoes & other garden produce, wheat, rice & turnips and any other produce, with HAMMAT paying to thrush the wheat & rice. WINTERS agrees to work the land well and tend the crops and run fence between the land of Giles TILLETT & James GARDNER.

Bond of $100 each to perform the agreement. Wt: Isaac LAROWE, Rich'd. H. HENDERSON.

Bk:Pg: 01:330 Date: 26 June 1825

James HAMILTON of Loudoun to Otho R. BEATTY and Samuel STERRETT of Leesburg. Bargain and sale of 2/3 interest in slave woman Lucy and her children Harriett, Maria, William and Lewis. Witness: Geo. LEE.

Bk:Pg: 01:331 – 01:332 Date: 29 March 1798

Adam HOUGHMAN/HOOFMAN & wife Mary of Loudoun to Philip FRY of Loudoun. Assignment of lease on 130a. Bryan FAIRFAX Gent. of Fairfax granted lease for lives on 1 May 1789 to Benjamin YATES of Loudoun (and sons Robert and James) who assigned it to HOUGHMAN. Witness: James LEITH, Samuel SKINNER, Thos. CHINN Junr. *Proven 9 October 1805 by James LEITH & Samuel SKINNER.*

Bk:Pg: 01:333 – 01:334 Date: 3 February 1773

Daniel HOOFHINTZ of Berks Co. Pa who survived John ROUS to John DUNLAP of Loudoun. Assignment of lease on 150a in Loudoun. John BURK late of said co. being seised as tenant for lives by deed of 5 October 1768 sold his interest to ROUS and HOOFHINTZ. ROUS is since dead. Witness: C. ROGERS, Chas. BINNS, Henry LANDON. *Proven 23 March 1773 by Charles BINNS.*

Bk:Pg: 01:335 Date: 11 October 1803

Matthew HARRISON to Richard COOMES/COMBS of Nelson Co. Kentucky. Bargain and sale of interest of Cuthbert HARRISON's moiety. Matthew HARRISON & his late brother Cuthbert HARRISON owned 1000a on Simpsons creek in said county of which they gave some to Isaac HOLE. Cuthbert sold his part to Hezekiah MURPHEY and MURPHEY sold to COOMES. Witness: J. LYONS, Samuel HOUGH, Jno. MATHIAS.

Bk:Pg: 01:336 – 01:337 Date: 13 September 1784

Thomas HUTTON of Washington Co. Pa to Thomas DAVIS of Loudoun. Assignment of lease on 134a. George Wm. FAIRFAX of Fairfax C. on 12 September 1765 leased to HUTTON. Witness: Thomas HAGUE, Amos HAGUE, Saml. THOMPSON, Amos JOLLIFFE, John POTTS. 9 October 1791 HATTON acknowledged in presence of Joshua GIST, Samuel CLANDINEN, Samuel THOMPSON, John PAIN? *Proven 10 April 1792 by Samuel THOMPSON.*

Bk:Pg: 01:338 – 01:340 Date: 17 May 1804

Lydia HOUGH of Loudoun to Jonathan CONRAD of Loudoun. Bargain and sale of 50a. Witness: [torn] 8 October 1804 pd by James HAMILTON. 13 May 1804 proven by Isaac HUFF. *Proven 8 October 1804 by James HAMILTON & 13 May 1803* [1805?] *by Isaac HUFF.*

Bk:Pg: 01:341 – 01:342 Date: 17 March 1806

David HIXSON of Loudoun to William PAXSON of Loudoun. Bond – David sold William his undivided right (1/8th part, about 28a) of the plantation on which his father formerly lived and will produce a deed whenever necessary. Witness: W. S. NEALE, Richard GRIFFITH, Israel H. THOMPSON. 12 May 1806 proven by Wm. S. NEALE & R'd. GRIFFITH.

Bk:Pg: 01:343 Date: 6 December 1799

Joseph HIXSON & wife Charlotte of Loudoun to William WRIGHT of Loudoun. Bargain and sale of undivided right (about 27a) of his father William HIXSON's landed estate. Not to interfere with Joseph's mother Alice HIXSON during her lifetime. Witness: Josh. DANNIEL, Asa HARRISS. *Proven 14 Jul 1800 by Josh DANIEL & proven 13 February 1804 by Asa HARRIS.*

Bk:Pg: 01:344 – 01:345 Date: ___ 1778

Henry HOWDERSHELT & wife Elizabeth of Loudoun to George ADOR. Assignment of lease on 101a where Henry now lives. Lease for lives dated 21 December 1773 from Thomas Ludwell LEE of Stafford Co. Va to Henry HOWDERSHELT (Philip HOWDERSHELT & Christian HOWDERSHELT). Witness: Richard GREEN, Jacob CALOR, Conrod WAGNER. *Proven 14 September 1778 by Richard GREEN & Jacob CALOR.*

Bk:Pg: 01:346 Date: 9 October 1787

Henry JENKINS & Thos. KENNAN to Isaac McBRIDE. Bond for injunction in chancery.

Bk:Pg: 01:346 [bottom] Date: 11Jan 1790

Bond from James JENKINS & James CLEVELAND to Bryan FAIRFAX for amount owed in decree of Court.

Bk:Pg: 01:347 Date: 12 August 1768

John JACOBS and William ELLZEY to Jacob SHILLING. Bond for injunction in chancery.

Bk:Pg: 01:347 [bottom] Date: 24 June 1794

Rec'd of Clerk of Loudoun the original deed LEE to TRUBBERVILLE which deed is to be returned when Mr. TRUBBERVILLE has made use of it. Signed Sam LAMKIN.

Bk:Pg: 01:348 – 01:349 Date: 9 October 1797

Timothy HIXSON & wife Elleanor of Loudoun to Benjamin HIXSON Junr. of Loudoun. Bargain and sale of 180a in Harrison Co. Va granted Timothy by patent dated 13 May 1790. Witness: Raynolds W. KELLISON, Cornelius SHAWEN. Certificate of examination of Elleanor and acknowledged by Timothy dated 13 October 1797.

Bk:Pg: 01:350 – 01:351 Date: 8 March 1841

Articles of agreement between Jacob L. GILLISPEY and Susan W. BENNETT. About to be married and Susan has considerable personal estate and entitled to other personal estate. She will not be subject to any of his debts, executions, judgments or claims. He will make full settlement of all of the mentioned property, etc. in trust for her use. 9 March 1841 acknowledged by Jacob L. GILLESPEY.

Bk:Pg: 01:352 – 01:353 Date: 18 October 1830

William GREGG of Loudoun to Enoch GARRETT of Loudoun. GREGG by agreement with his brother, sisters & mother dated 13 August 1829 he sold the personal property of his father Joseph GREGG dec'd without administration being entered into with a condition to apply the proceeds of sale to discharge the debts and now to satisfy the parties the money from the sale shall be strictly applied to that purpose. Trust using all he is entitled to inherit from his father's estate for his faithful performance. Witness: N. C. WILLIAMS, Josiah GREGG, Thomas EWERS, Townsend J. JURY. 31 October 1831 proven by Ths. EWERS & Townsend JURY as to GREGG.

Bk:Pg: 01:354 – 01:355 Date: 1 January 1799

Abel GARRETT of Loudoun to Leven LUCKETT of Loudoun. Bargain and sale of 100a granted Abel by his father Thomas GARRETT by deed of 8 January 1790. Witness: Rawleigh CHINN, Leven POWELL, Thomas CHINN, Richard CHINN. *Proven 9 April 1799 by Leven POWELL & Rawleigh CHINN.*

Bk:Pg: 01:356 – 01:359 Date: 18 April 1845

Ryland T. JACOBS of 1st part, James B. WILSON of 2nd part and Wm. CHAMBLIN, Gourley REEDER, John B. HEREFORD & Theodore LEITH of 3rd part. Trust for debt to third parties using farm animals and items, crops, household items. Witness: J. LEMON?, M. P. WATSON, H. M. DAVIS.

Bk:Pg: 01:360 – 01:361 Date: 1 October 1845
Edward B. JENKINS & wife Martha of Loudoun to Dr. James WEEKS of Aldie. Bargain and sale of 92a from larger tract where JENKINS now lives, adj Amos FERGUSON, Joseph PILES (reserving the privilege of cutting the pine trees and bushes from ½ of the Pine Grove). Certificate of examination for Martha returned 25 October 1845 by French SIMPSON, John MOORE

Bk:Pg: 01:362 Date: 5 May 1849
George JACOBS to Thomas SANDERS Sheriff of Loudoun. JACOBS took benefit of act of Insolvent Debtors under a writ of capias by John JONES Jr. ass'ee of Jonathan CONARD, surrendered all interest in 3a between Short Hill and Blue Ridge (where George now resides) conveyed by him to John MILLER in trust to secure payment due to Rynard JACOBS.

Bk:Pg: 01:363 – 01:367 Date: 10 November 1845
Samuel A. JACKSON of Loudoun now in Washington DC to Berkeley WARD of Fauquier Co. Trust for debt to Catherine E. WILLIAMS of Washington DC using "Scotland Mills" adj ___ JAMES. Witness: W. THOMPSON, Benjamin R. MORSELL.

Bk:Pg: 01:368 – 01:369 Date: 14 September 1818
George JOHNSON to Isaac YOUNG. Lease of tract where JOHNSON now lives for term of 8 years. Two of the children of Archibald YOUNG dec'd with [torn] widow said JOHNSON has intermarried and attain their ages before the expiration of the 8 years (if neither claim or get possession of their shares then out of the first rents due after the expiration of said 8 years said Isaac to be reimbursed in proportion to their shares). YOUNG to keep the land after the 8 years during the continuance of the estate JOHNSON at the rent of $160/year. Witness: William O. CHAPPELEAR, Charles McKNIGHT, Ann CHAPPELEAR.

Bk:Pg: 01:370 – 01:371 Date: 20 January 1827
Richard S. JONES of Loudoun of 1st part, John SIMPSON of Loudoun of 2nd part and James TAVENNER Snr. of 3rd part. Bond with TAVENNER as his security payable to Thomas ROGERS Admr. of Isaiah POTTS using slaves Jo. Hannah and her child Linny & an infant not named. Witness: Thomas ROGERS, George CARTER, John WHITE.

Bk:Pg: 01:372 – 01:374 Date: 10 November 1826
Yearsley JONES of Loudoun to Seth SMITH of Loudoun. JONES indebted to sundry persons in Loudoun for more than his property

worth. Trust using one horse (bought of David SIMPSON) and to sell property in schedule (horses, crops, household items, farm items). SMITH to collect and apply proceeds to the payments. Witness: John WEADON, Fielder BURCH.

Bk:Pg: 01:375 – 01:376 Date: 24 June 1816
John JOHNSON of Loudoun to Phinehas THOMAS of Loudoun. Bargain and sale of remainder of tract granted to JOHNSON by patent for 30a that is left after the recovery of Rebecca ROMINE &c by suit in Court, adj HANBY's patent, ___ LEE, Williams Gap branch, HOLSCLAW's patent. Witness: Calvin THATCHER, David LOVETT, Robt. CHINN.

Bk:Pg: 01:377 Date: 23 October 1816
William JONES & Elizabeth JONES of Jefferson Co. Va bound to William PAXSON of Loudoun. JONESes sold PAXSON all their interest in 5a on Blue Ridge and also the mill and lot annexed formerly occupied by Thomas CATON, conveyed to CATON by William JONES dec'd and by CATON to said PAXSON. JONESes to provide deed for said lotts. Witness: Jonas POTTS, Wm. MONROE, Wm. PAXSON, Jr.

Bk:Pg: 01:378 – 01:380 Date: 27 March 1771
William JONES of Loudoun to John GRIFFITH of Loudoun. Bargain and sale of two contiguous tracts (190a and 55a) where GRIFFITH now lives. Witness: James JONES, Jabez JONES, Jon'a. PRICE. Release of dower by wife Mary.

Bk:Pg: 01:381 Date: 1 August 1825
John WHITE & Craven OSBURN Justices of the Peace of Loudoun certify that Sarah IDEN wife of Samuel IDEN acknowledged deed of conveyance of real estate to Westley SEARS dated 11 June 1825. Rec'd 8 August 1825. [see below]

Bk:Pg: 01:382 – 01:384 Date: 11 June 1825
Samuel IDEN & wife Sarah of Loudoun to Wesley SEARS of Loudoun. Bargain and sale of 2a adj Stacy TAYLOR, Moses DILLON, Henry GREGG. Witness: William NICKOLS, Henry S. TAYLOR. Certificate of examination of Sarah returned 1 August 1825 by Craven OSBURN, John WHITE. [also see above]

Bk:Pg: 01:385 Date: 30 March 1813
Certificate of examination for Margaret JOHNSON wife of William JOHNSON for deed to William NEWTON for bargain and sale of 75a returned 30 March 1813 by Wm. B. HARRISON, Samuel MURREY.

Bk:Pg: 01:386 – 01:388 Date: 15 March 1806
Benjamin JAMES & wife Mary of Loudoun to Andrew REDMOND of Loudoun. Bargain and sale of 28a in Loudoun granted to Elijah MAJOR by deed from proprietors office on the old part of the old mountain road. Witness: James SPENCER, Benj. REDMOND, Emmor REES.

Bk:Pg: 01:389 – 01:390 Date: 15 September 1812
Price JACOBS of Loudoun to Wm. BRONAUGH of Loudoun. Trust for debt to John DUNKIN using 61a. Witness: Moses BROWN, Ben. GRAYSON, Aaron BURSON, Samuel DUNKIN.

Bk:Pg: 01:391 – 01:392 Date: 6 December 1799
John JOHNSON of Loudoun to Wm. GORE of Loudoun. Trust for debt to John SCATTERDAY using __a (a vacancy which JOHNSON has levied a land warrant on) adj Tholomiah RHODES, Martin OVERFIELD. Witness: Archabald McNEALE, Peggy HESKETT, Martin OVERFIELD, Elizabeth OVERFIELD.

Bk:Pg: 01:392 [bottom] Date: 7 April 1796
William JEANES. Deed of emancipation for negro man formerly slave to me called Fortin. Witness: Elyndor JEANS, Charles SMITH.

Bk:Pg: 01:393 – 01:396 Date: 11 May 1824
Thomas KIDWELL & wife Elizabeth of 1st part, Robert MOFFETT of 2nd part, and Jacob SHRIVER of 3rd part, all of Loudoun. SHRIVER stands bound as security for KIDWELL on bonds on which judgment & execution are awarded, one at suit of Geo. F. THORNTON use of Jno. M. McCARTY and the other at suit of Wm. KING and is also bound as his appearance bail in suit of Wm. KING ass'ee use of Jno. GRAY in Superior Ct. Trust using 50a conveyed to KIDWELL by Edmund J. LEE & wife Sally 13 September 1822 (Deed Book 3F, page 023); 25a conveyed to KIDWELL by John MATHIAS 2 February 1817 (Deed Book 2W, page 315); 11a conveyed to KIDWELL by MATTHIAS 26 June 1818 (Deed Book 2X, page 363); 47a being the residue of a lot of 87a conveyed to KIDWELL by MATTHIAS after taking off 40a sold by KIDWELL to SHRIVER. Witness: Samuel EDWARDS, Alfred A. ESKRIDGE, B. SHREVE Jr., Jno. J. MATTHIAS. Certificate of examination of Elizabeth returned 11 May 1824 by Ebenezer GRUBB, John WHITE. *Proven 12 June 1824 by Benjamin SHREVE & Alfred ESKRIDGE.*

Bk:Pg: 01:397 – 01:398 Date: 29 August 1822
Nicholas KILE & wife Mary of Loudoun to Epamenondas M. LANE of Loudoun. Bargain and sale of interest to lot in Loudoun which was purchased by Nicholas KILE from Col. Joseph LANE dec'd. Witness:

Wm. BRONAUGH, George KILE, W. C. PALMER, Norval CHAMBLIN. Certificate of examination for Mary returned 21 October 1822 by Wm. BRONAUGH, Francis W. LUCKETT. *Proven 9 June 1823 by George KILE & No[r]val CHAMBLIN.*

Bk:Pg: 01:399 – 01:401 Date: 1 November 1826
Thomas KIDWELL & wife Elizabeth of Loudoun to James B. SPENCE of Loudoun. Bargain and sale of 6a adj Jno. CUNARD. Edmond J. LEE of Alexandria holds a deed of trust on the lot and with John J. MATHIAS a trustee release the trust. Witness: E. GRUBB.

Bk:Pg: 01:402 – 01:404 Date: 2 January 1796
John KEINE and Newton KEINE of Northumberland Co. Va to Thomas WREN and William WREN tenants in common of Loudoun. Bargain and sale of Lot No. 112 in Centerville adj KEINE. Witness: James Lane TRIPLETT, Isaac HUTCHINSON, Jonathan GOLDRING. *Proven by Isaac HUTCHISON 8 February 1796 & on 8 May 1797 by James TRIPLETT.*

Bk:Pg: 01:405 Date: 10 May 1799
Osburn KING of Loudoun to William WHALEY. Bill of sale for horse, household items. Witness: John CARTER, Thos. E. MINOR.

Bk:Pg: 01:406 – 01:407 Date: 21 September 1787
Joshua KNOWLS/KNOWLES of Loudoun to John HENRY Junior of Loudoun. Assignment of lease of 100a adj John SCHOOLY, Wm. WILDMAN. George Wm. FAIRFAX Esqr. of Fairfax granted lease for lives dated 3 September 1765 to Joshua KNOWLS (and Elisha SCHOOLY and William SCHOOLY sons of John SCHOOLY). Witness: John CUMMINGS, William HIXSON, Jacob SHERB. Also signed by wife Jemimah KNOWLS.

Bk:Pg: 01:408 – 01:409 Date: 10 November 1804
Robert KIRK & wife Sarah of Alexandria Va to Benjamin Hough CANBY of Loudoun. Bargain and sale of 3a adj Leesburg on west side, __ AWBREY, __ FOSTER, __ BERRY, __ LITTLEJOHN. Witness: A. SUTHERLAND, Richard GRIFFITH, Thos. SWANN, Arch McCLEAN.

Bk:Pg: 01:410 – 01:412 Date: 25 September 1809
Mary Ann KELLY & Edward KELLY of Loudoun to Israel LACEY & Charles B. MERCER of Loudoun. Trust to secure James MONROE Exor of late Judy JONES using slaves Charles, Tom, Joe & Stephen. Witness: Asher PULLEN, James LEACH, Alexander LACEY.

Bk:Pg: 01:413 Date: ?? October 1783 [in crease]

Robert KIRKPATRICK of Loudoun. Power of attorney to friend Isaac VANDEVANTER of Loudoun to recover money from Jacob JACOBS, Saml. GARDNER, Benj. HUGHSTON, Edward HOLMES, Jacob and John MOORE. Witness: John DODD, Josh. DANNIEL. Proven ___ by Joshua DANIEL.

Bk:Pg: 01:414 – 01:417 Date: 2 April 1804

Robert William KIRK & wife Sarah of Alexandria District of Columbia to William SMITH of Loudoun. Bargain and sale of part of Lot No. ___ in Leesburg at Market and Back Streets. Witness: R. J. TAYLOR, [torn], Thos. SWANN. Ack'd. by Robert in Philadelphia 2 January 1808. Also Certificate of examination for Sarah returned 2 April 1804 by Jacob HOFFMAN, Cuthbert POWELL. *Proven 11 January 1800* [??] *by Thomas SWANN.*

Bk:Pg: 01:418 Date: 31 March 1823

Alice KENT of Loudoun to William H. DORSEY of Loudoun. Bargain and sale of ¼a (purchased of Benjamin KENT) adj DORSEY where he now resides, Thornton WALKER. Witness: Willis TRIPLETT, Mahlon BALDWIN, John HANN, Elias KENT, Craven WALKER, Geo. E. LLOYD.

Bk:Pg: 01:419 – 01:422 Date: 17 March 1792

William LEE Esqr. of James City to Thomas KEEN (and William KEENE son of Francis KEENE and Oliver SIMPSON son of George SIMPSON) of Loudoun. Lease for lives of 155a adj John BROWN, Bull Run. Witness: John HUTCHISON, Chs. [creased], Reuben HUTCHISON, Elijah HUTCHISON, George LEWIS. Signed by Jeremiah COCKERILL for Wm. LEE. 11 April 1809 proven by Elias LACEY & o. c. & 9 Oct parties proved by John HUTCHISON Jr. 5 October 1808 claim assigned by Thos. KEEN to John SCHOLFIELD. Witness: John FULTON, John HUTCHISON Jr., Elias LACEY. *Proven 11 April 1809 by Elias LACEY.*

Bk:Pg: 01:423 Date: 5 May 1810

Sarah KEYES of Jefferson Co. Va to Thomas WHITE of Loudoun. Bill of sale for negro woman and child named Betty and Hester. Betty is about 28y old and Hester 2y old. Witness: William OGDON, John WHITE, Lucrecia P. WHITE.

Bk:Pg: 01:424 Date: 6 Jul 1798

Reynolds KELISON of Loudoun to Henry HUFF of Loudoun. Bill of sale for grain. Witness: John SAGER, Peter STOCK, John BAYSE. *Proven 9 Jul 1798 by Henry HUFF.*

Bk:Pg: 01:425 Date: 9 June 1800 in Leesburgh

I will thank you to send me by some safe hand to Alex'a. three deeds left in your office for Rever'd. Mr. FAIRFAX & Henry LEE to Wm. WILSON & myself that they may be there certified & returned for record. If no opportunity offers before Col. POWELL will take charge of them. Yours John POTTS.

Bk:Pg: 01:425 [bottom] Date: ___

Mr. BLINCOE is requested to deliver to Mr. JONES the deed of trust from H. LEE to Walter JONES for the benefit of J. D. ORR. Signed C. BINNS.

Bk:Pg: 01:426 – 01:427 Date: 6 September 1788

Richard Bland LEE of Loudoun to William AMBLER (and his sons William & Vincent) of Loudoun. Lease for lives of 136a. Witness: Theodorick LEE, William B'd. SEARS, John BRAGG, William BALLENGER. *Proven 13 October 1788 by William BALLENGER & John BRAGG.*

Bk:Pg: 01:428 – 01:429 Date: 17 May 1798

Ludwell LEE to Benjamin THOMAS (and wife Margaret and son Marcus). Lease for lives of 124a adj John JENKINS, Horsepen Run. Witness: Johnston CLEVELAND, Basil STONESTREET, John NORRIS, Jacob WILDEN Senr.

Bk:Pg: 01:430 Date: 12 June 1818

Agreement to rent of James B. LANE trustee for Newton KEENE the place on which I now live for the next ensuing three years commencing 1 Jan next and ending last of December 1821. I bind myself not to cut any green wood except what may be absolutely necessary for repairs. I further bind myself to have the farm & houses in good order & repaired at the end of the three years. Signed Robert P. LANHAM. Witness: Johnston CLEVELAND, Elizabeth ROSE, Richard ROSE.

Bk:Pg: 01:431 – 01:432 Date: 5 December 1820

William H. LANE & wife Sarah of Burlington, Lawrence Co. Ohio to Benjamin BRIDGES of Loudoun. Bargain and sale of undivided 1/9th interest as heir of Hardage LANE dec'd late of Montgomery Co. Md in tract now in possession of John HAVENER. Land was not included in division of the lands belonging to said Hardage in Va. Witness: John H. DUFFEY, John STANHOPE, [illegible name] *Proven 14 May 1821 by John H. DUFFEY & John STANHOPE.*

Bk:Pg: 01:433 – 01:434 Date: 29 February 1828
John LAMBAUGH of Loudoun to Abba ANDERSON of Loudoun. Bargain and sale of 1a that John purchased of Presley SAUNDERS and SAUNDERS purchased from Francis TRIPLETT in the suburbs of Leesburg between the lots of a free man of colour named Isaac and a lot sold by TRIPLETT to a free man of colour Jacob WILLIAMS but now owned by Genl. George RUST. [no witness signatures]

Bk:Pg: 01:435- 01:438 Date: __ January 1805
Sebastian LOSH & wife Jane LOSH late Jane McINTIRE and formerly widow and relict of Alexander McINTIRE now dec'd of Loudoun to Benjamin H. CANBY of Leesburg. Release of dower claim on ¾a nr Leesburg adj "Cavans' Meadow" and the lot formerly sold by Daniel McINTIRE late of Loudoun but now of Kentucky to Thomas FRANCIS of Loudoun which lot by Alexander McINTIRE in his will devised to his son Charles McINTIRE since dec'd as well also that ½a by Alexander's will devised to his son William now of Loudoun. Witness: Fleet SMITH, Christ'o. ROPER. *Proven 10 September 1805 by Christian* [Christopher] *ROPER.*

Bk:Pg: 01:439 – 01:442 Date: 7 September 1820
William H. LANE now of Leesburg to Sampson BLINCOE of Leesburg. Thomas GASSAWAY of Leesburg on ___ 1820 became appearance bail for LANE at suit of Adam LYNN in Superior Ct. Trust to indemnify GASSAWAY using lot in Leesburg at intersection of Cornwall and King Sts. adj William KLINE. Witness: Wm. TEMPLETON, Wm. SEEDERS, John M. DREAN. 26 February 1821 proven by Wm. SEEDERS.

Bk:Pg: 01:443 – 01:446 Date: 8 March 1829
Mesheck LACEY of 1st part, Lemuel HUTCHISON of 2nd part and John HUTCHISON of 3rd part. LACEY indebted to John HUTCHISON. Trust to Lemuel using the entire lotts in Middleburg whereon the dwelling house where LACEY resides together with his hatter's shop, and slaves Peter his blacksmith & wife Charlott, Emily, Francis, and the two youngest children of Charlott. Witness: Beverly HUTCHISON, Thomas LATHAM, Edwin ROGERS. 9 March 1829 ackn'd by Jno. HUTCHISON & Lemual HUTCHISON & proven by Beverly HUTCHISON as to LACEY.

Bk:Pg: 01:447 – 01:450 Date: 22 October 1807
Whitman LEITH of Loudoun to William VICKERS of Loudoun. Mortgage of 70a where LEITH resides being the residue of 100a conveyed to him by Elisha POWELL after deducting the 30a which was formerly conveyed by LEITH to VICKERS. Witness: Amos

JOHNSON, B. E. WILLS, Gustavus HARRISON, Burr POWELL. 14 December 1807 proven by Amos JOHNSTON & Burr POWELL. 13 February 1809 fully proven by Gustavus HARRISON and ordered to be recorded. *Recorded Liber 2K, folio 203.* 3 May 1809 William VICKERS relinquished all claim as fully satisfied. Witness: John SINCLAIR, Abraham BROWN, A. GIBSON.

Bk:Pg: 01:451 – 01:452 Date: 21 November 1801

Articles of agreement between Isaac LEWIS and James LEWIS and Reuben GOREHAM/GREHAM to let GOREHAM lease the field for seven of ten years. Witness: Theophilus REES, William GREHAM.

Bk:Pg: 01:453 – 01:455 Date: 19 November 1826

Elizabeth LEACHMAN and Dorothy Ann commonly called Dolly Ann LEACHMAN of 1st part, Burr W. HARRISON of 2nd part, and William GULICK of 3rd part. LEACHMANs are indebted to William CARR with GULICK as security on the note dated 6 February 1826. Trust using slave Mahala aged about 14y. Witness: Amos GULICK, Saml. TRIPLETT, James P. LOVETT.

Bk:Pg: 01:456 – 01:457 Date: ___ 18__

Leven LUCKET Exor. of Francis H. PEYTON of Loudoun to Henry SETTLE of Loudoun. Release of mortgage dated 10 November 1812. [no signature or witnesses.]

Bk:Pg: 01:458 – 01:459 Date: 29 March 1821

Sarah LACEY of Loudoun to Lucinda L. RICE (daughter of Jesse RICE & wife Thirza). Bill of sale (reserving an estate for my life) of negro man slave Pompy, household items, farm animals. Witness: S. BLINCOE, Thos. MORELLEE. *Proven 20 March 1821 by S. BLINCOE.*

Bk:Pg: 01:460 Date: 15 April 1815

Thomas LEEDOM & wife Hannah and Jesse THOMAS & wife Elizabeth sole heirs to estate of Israel WILLIAMS dec'd, all of Loudoun, to William and James THOMPSON of Loudoun. Bargain and sale of ½ of estate of David WILLIAMS dec'd. Israel WILLIAMS was heir to 1/4th of estate of David WILLIAMS dec'd. Israel in 1791 purchased of Thomas WILLIAMS all his right in estate of David WILLIAMS dec'd both real and personal. David possessed a lease on 169a whereon he resided and whereon Margaret HEMPBURN now lives. Witness: Joseph THOMAS, Edward CUNARD Junr., Bennit MARKS. *Proven 14 August 1815 by Joseph THOMAS & Edward CUNNARD.*

Bk:Pg: 01:461 – 01:462 Date: 13 March 1785

Adam LONG of Loudoun to Charles HANSFORD. Assignment of lease of 100a. Thomas Ludwell LEE Esqr. granted lease for lives on 21 December 1773 during lives of John DAWSON 3rd son, Charles DAWSON 4th son and Henrietta 5th daughter of John DAWSON. Witness: John SNIDER, Conrad BITZER, John LEASE. *Proven 13 March 1786 by John SNIDER & John LEASE.*

Bk:Pg: 01:463 – 01:464 Date: 4 November 1776

Maj. James LANE of Cameron Parish to John ORR of Cameron Parish. Lease for lives of 275a "Bull Run Tract" (to LANE by Robert CARTER Esqr. 4 November 1757 on three lives chosen by Enoch GRIGESBEY). Witness: Chs. ESKRIDGE, William MITCHELL, Benjamin MITCHELL. *Proven 14 April 1777 by William & Benjamin MITCHELL.*

Bk:Pg: 01:465 – 01:466 Date: 6 September 1804

William LOCKER, tavern keeper of Loudoun to William JINKINS, planter of Loudoun. Bill of sale for all goods and chattels of whatever nature which LOCKER now possessed except wearing apparel. Witness: John JENKINS, Hendson JENKINS. *Proven 10 September 1804 by John JENKINS.*

Bk:Pg: 01:467 – 01:468 Date: 11 June 1765

Charles LEWIS of Loudoun to John PILES of Loudoun. Lease of 16½a adj PILES, LEWIS, ___ PEARSON. Witness: W. ELLZEY, John MINOR, John GRIFFITH.

Bk:Pg: 01:469 – 01:470 Date: 12 June 1765

Charles LEWIS of Loudoun to John PILES of Loudoun. Release of 16½a adj PILES, LEWIS, ___ PEARSON, ___ ELLZEY. Witness: W. ELLZEY, John GRIFFITH, [torn]

Bk:Pg: 01:471 – 01:472 Date: 28 October 1803

William LEACH, Hezekiah B. LEACH and James LEACH sons of John LEACH dec'd and Hezekiah ODEN who intermarried with Elizabeth LEACH daughter of said John LEACH dec'd and Mary LEACH daughter of said John LEACH having been informed that it was the wish of their father that his two youngest daughters Ann and Susanna should have over and above an equal proportion of his estate, two small negroes, Mary about 4y old and Isaac about 2y old. Give up all their claim to the negroes and will take an equal proportion of the balance of their father's estate, who died intestate. Witness: Jas. Lewis GIBBS Senr., Moses DOWDELL, Sarah LEACH. 13 February 1804 proven by Moses DOUDLE as to James LEATCH, Mary LEATCH and Hezekiah B. LEACH.

Bk:Pg: 01:473 – 01:474 Date: 15 February 1802

Willis LEGG of Loudoun to Allen DAVIS. Bill of sale for horse. Witness: Israel LACEY, Henry BRAWNER, Thos. BEVERIDGE. Proven 14 September 1802 by Israel LACY and ordered to be certified.

Bk:Pg: 01:475 Date: 21 December 1804

Isaac LEWIS of Loudoun by Susannah BUTCHER (Power of attorney from Isaac dated 16 November 1804) of Loudoun to Jacob LEWIS of Loudoun. Bargain and sale of moiety or ½ of Grist Mill and 1/3 of fulling Mill. Witness: Wm. BRONAUGH, Ben. GRAYSON, Joseph DAVIS. *Proven 9 April 1803* [1805?] *by William BRONAUGH.*

Bk:Pg: 01:476 Date: 28 October 1806

Isaac LEWIS and James LEWIS of Shelby Co. KY to Benjamin GRAYSON of Loudoun. Power of attorney to sell tract in Loudoun adj Benjamin OVERFIELD, Samuel TORBERT, Peter ROMINE, Martin OVERFIELD, and now in possession & occupation of Rewben GRAHAM which was sold to Isaac & James by Benjamin OVERFIELD. Witness: Thomas BARTON, Benjamin GRAYSON Jr., John HENDRICKS, Junr. *Proven 11 May 1807 by John HENDRICKS.*

Bk:Pg: 01:477 – 01:478 Date: 7 April 1798

William LANE 3rd of Loudoun to friend William LANE Junr. of Loudoun. Power of attorney to collect money debts and enact suits. Witness: Wm. GUNNELL Jr, Humphry PEAKE. Proven 10 April 1798 by Wm. GUNNELL. *Recorded Deed Book Y, page 211.*

Bk:Pg: 01:479 Date: 7 June 1782

William LANE Jr. to William WRIGHT. Bargain and sale of 3a where WRIGHT now lives known by the name of "Wappin". Witness: T. DADE, H. POTTER. *Proven 10 February 1783 by H. POTTER.*

Bk:Pg: 01:480 Date: 18 March 1820

Wm. H. LANE obligates himself and heirs that his wife Sarah LANE shall on or before 1 July next relinquish to David OGDEN all her right of dower to land which he sells to OGDEN this day. Witness: S. BLINCOE, Thos. MORALLEE. *Proven 23 March 1820 by Thomas MORALLEE.*

Bk:Pg: 01:481 – 01:482 Date: 4 April 1801

James LEATH of Loudoun to Jonathan McVEIGH of Loudoun. Lease of 50a on Goose Creek adj MONTEITH. Witness: Saml. BOGGESS, A. GIBSON, Jesse McVEIGH, Robert WHITACRE. *Proven 13 April 1801 by James LEITH & Jesse McVEIGH.*

Bk:Pg: 01:483 Date: ___

Isaac LAROWE of Loudoun to John HALLING of Loudoun. Trust for slaves Nancy, Kitty, Henry & John to repay $207.50 by 1 Jan next. Witness: Benj. SHREVE, Chs. ELGIN. *Proven 14 March 1812 by Charles ELGIN.*

Bk:Pg: 01:484 – 01:486 Date: 2 November 1785

William LANE & wife Susanna to Samuel TALBOTT. Bargain and sale of 105a in Cameron Parish on Little Rockey Run (part of tract purchased of William & John JOHNSTON) adj ___ NESBITT, David BOYD dec'd., William BUCKLEY, Mrs. Barbary BERKLEY. Witness: William READ, Charles DAVIS, Beatis DORSEY.

Bk:Pg: 01:487 – 01:490 Date: 26 November 1808

Hugh LEMON of Frederick Co. Md to James RUSSELL of Waterford. Bargain and sale of 1a near Waterford purchased by Edward DORSEY from Mahlon JANNEY and sold by DORSEY to LEMON. Witness: Stephen WILSON, Elizabeth WILSON, Merab SCOTT. *Proven 10 Jul 1809 by Stephen & Elizabeth WILSON.*

Bk:Pg: 01:491 Date: 8 March 1814

Israel LACEY of Loudoun to friend Letty PALMER of Loudoun. Lending her farm animals and items, household items, to cease at death of LACEY. Witness: Lewis M. SMITH, John HENDRICKS, Jacob Lynge COLVIG. *Proven 14 March 1814 by Lewis SMITH.*

Bk:Pg: 01:492 – 01:495 Date: 12 March 1810

Augustine LOVE & wife Mary of Loudoun to William P. HALE of Mason Co. Bargain and sale of 88a on Goose Creek adj Danl. BROWN, Brown's Mill road, road from Coe's Mill, road leading to Vernon's Fulling Mill. Witness: A. GIBSON, Hugh SMITH, Noble BEVERIDGE, Mesheck LACEY. Certificate of examination for Mary returned 12 March 1810 signed by Leven LUCKETT, Wm. BRONAUGH. 10 September 1810 p'd by Abner GIBSON. 21 September 1837 proven by H. SMITH.

Bk:Pg: 01:496 – 01:497 Date: 11 February 1811

David LACY & wife Sarah of Loudoun to John MINES of Loudoun. Bargain and sale of 10¾a adj LACY's patent. Witness: John LINTON, William HAWLING, John HAWLING, S. WHERRY.

Bk:Pg: 01:498 – 01:499 Date: 25 September 1824

James LAWRUE & wife Elizabeth of Ohio to Eli McKNIGHT of Loudoun. Bargain and sale of 35a adj ___ LOVETT, ___ BROWN. Witness: Charles CHAMBLIN, Wm. McKNIGHT, Eli McKNIGHT, Ezekiel EMERSON, Catharine STIRES. 14 May 1828 in Ohio – Elisebeth LARROW widow acknowledged conveyance was voluntary.

Bk:Pg: 01:500 Date: 31 May 1833

To Lewis F. MANKIN, John SWART & Lewis GRIGSBY, freeholders of Loudoun. Henry LOWE of Loudoun has this day given information to me Wm. B. HARRISON Justice of the Peace for Loudoun that he hath taken up an estray colt, any of the three to view and appraise estray. Viewed and valued on 31 May 1833 by the three first listed.

Bk:Pg: 01:501 – 01:505 Date: 9 May 1785

A list of the taxable property in Thomas LEWIS's district taken by Hardage LANE April 1785.

Numbers: free males >21y, Negroes >16y, Negroes <16y, horses, no. cattle

Robert ATHY 1-0-0-2-2
Terrence BURNS, Negro Daniel 1-0-1-2-3
John BURNS 1-0-0-2-3
William BUTCHER, Negro Baker 1-1-0-6-10
Nathaniel BARKER, Negro Harry 1-1-0-5-7
William BARKER 1-0-0-4-4
Charles BRENT, William BRENT, n's. Ned, Beck, Bett, Kate, Hannah, Sarah, Joshua, Tom, Frank, [creased] 2-6-4-6-11
Nathaniel BARKER Junr. 1-0-0-2-3
Henry BUTLER, N. Rose 1-0-1-1-0
Mary BARKER, N's. Moll, Harry, Charles 0-1-2-3-4
Samuel BARKER 1-0-0-3-3
Sandford COCKERILL, N's. Stephen, Daniel, Rachel, George, Tom 1-3-2-4-6
Daniel COMBS 1-0-0-2-3
Allen DAVIS 1-0-0-4-5
Edward DAY, N's. Sampson, Charles 1-1-1-2-8
Zachariah DAY 1-0-0-1-1
William D'BELL, N's. Stephen, Dark, Arthur, Hannah, Daniel, Tom, Alice, Simon 1-3-5-6-10
John ELLZEY, N. Sarah 1-0-1-2-5
James EVERINGHAM 1-0-0-1-1
Elizabeth EVANS 0-0-0-2-3
Amos FOX, Edmund HERRING, Edward MADDEN 0-0-0-7-4
William FLETCHER 1-0-0-2-0

Luke FRIZEL, N's. Harry, Hannah, Sam, Grace, Mill, Cloe 1-2-4-4-7
Joseph GANT 1-0-0-5-5
Nicholas GRIMES, N's. Sam, Bristo, Sue, Sarah, Nan, Lott, Harry, Ruth, Dark, George, Jacob, Captain, Jack, Simon 1-6-8-6-18
William GRIMES, N. Daniel 1-0-1-2-4
William HALLEY (of Fairfax Co.), N's. Gerrard, George, Jane, Mill 0-4-0-0-0
Joshua HARRISON 1-0-0-5-4
John HEBBURNE, N's. Winney, Mime 1-1-1-3-2
Thomas Ellzey HARRISON 1-0-0-2-2
John HURST 1-0-0-2-3
John HOWELL 1-0-0-1-0
James HOPPER, Jesse WHARTON 2-0-0-5-7
Charles HUGULY, John CRISWELL 2-0-0-5-9
Jonathan JEWELL, William FLOYD 2-0-0-4-5
Stephen JENKINS 1-0-0-1-3
Aaron JENKINS 1-0-0-1-4
John JENKINS, John FITZGIBBIN, N's. Kate, Will, Daniel, Dick, Caleb 0-1-4-5-13
Susanna KITCHIN 0-0-0-2-2
William KITCHIN, N's. Jack, Fan, Abraham, Jude, Daniel, John 1-2-4-5-8
Daniel KITCHIN, N. Harry 1-0-1-2-0
Alexander KIDWELL, N's. Charles, Tom, Sall 1-1-2-2-1
Hardage LANE, Joseph EVERETT, Sanford RAMEY Junr., Dennis CROWLEY, N's. Moses, Cato, Nan, Bett, Betty, Anna, Hannah, Ellis, Peter, Cate, Nell, Winney, James, John, Heth, Jude, Abba 6-7-10-10-32
Daniel LEWIS, N's. Luce, Bristo, Charles, Jesse, John, Dick 1-1-5-7-13
Emanuel LAY, N. Rachel 1-0-1-3-9
Sarah LAY, N's. Will, Harry, Ned, June, Suck, Winney, Tom, Simon, Reuben, Dinah 0-6-3-4-12
Stephen LAY, N's. Hannah, Wallace, 1 stud horse 1-1-1-5-7
Daniel LEDGINGHAM 1-0-0-2-2
Abraham LAY Junr., N. Peter 1-1-0-5-10
Nicholas MONEY 1-0-0-4-8
Joseph McDERMENT, N. Edmund 1-1-0-2-3
Daniel NEALE 1-0-0-3-7
Sarah NEWELL 0-0-0-0-6
Randolph NOE, John HARRISON 2-0-0-3-13
Charles NEALE, N. Dinah 1-0-1-1-2
Christopher NEALE, N. Harry, Mime, Frank, Jack, Nan, Sall, Arthur, Sam 1-3-5-5-11
Eli OLIVER 1-0-0-1-1
John PASH, George HAND 2-0-0-2-3
Philip PORTER 1-0-0-3-2

Peter ROANY 1-0-0-0-0
John STONESTREET, N's. Saul, Jenny, Nace, Jude, Sam, Benjamin, Pat 1-2-5-4-5
Gideon SMITH 1-0-0-6-4
John SMITH 1-0-0-2-6
Enoch SMITH, N's. Nan, Sarah, Joe, Davy 1-1-3-6-10
John SKIRVIN 1-0-0-2-3
Leonard SMITH 1-0-0-0-0
James SANDERS 1-0-0-1-4
William STEPHENS 1-0-0-2-5
Davis STONE, N's. Will, Doll 1-0-0-2-5
Robert SCOTT, Thomas HOUGH, N's. Pris, Doll 2-1-1-5-6
Demovill TALBERT, N's. Joe, Sall, Tom 1-1-2-5-3
John THOMPSON 1-0-0-2-1
Richard THOMPSON 1-0-0-1-1
Thomas TAYLOR 1-0-0-2-4
George THOMAS, N's. Alice, Harry, Hannah, Phil 1-1-3-2-1
Cornelius VAUGHAN, N's. George, Hannah 1-1-1-5-9
Uriah VERMILLIAN 1-0-0-2-0
Leroy VAUGHAN 1-0-0-1-2
Richard WARDEN 1-0-0-2-3
James WELCH 1-0-0-1-1
Benjamin YATES 1-0-0-5-7

Bk:Pg: 01:506 – 01:508 Date: 6 November 1826

Benjamin MITCHEL, Martha MITCHEL, John CRANE, Elizabeth CRANE, Catharine JETT by Peter JETT her Guardian of Loudoun to John PURCELL of Loudoun. Bargain and sale of 13a on NW fork of Goose Creek adj Stephen E. ROSSEL, John HOUGH, John LASSWELL's tract of land now the Glebe land of Shelbourn Parish, Richard BROWN. Witness: Jos. L. CRAIN, Nicholas OSBURN, Daniel COCKERILL, Craven OSBURN. Acknowledged in Fauquier Co. by John CRAIN & wife Elizabeth CRAIN 19 March 1827 before James PICKETT, D. FAUNTLEROY.

Bk:Pg: 01:509 – 01:510 Date: 26 February 1780

Rhodom MOXLEY (Lieu'nt of the Second Virginia Reg'mt belonging to the Army of the U.S. of North America) to brother Wm. MOXLEY of Loudoun. Power of attorney - In case of his death gives all his lands or tenements due him as an officer in the Army, also all other property that he now or may hereafter possess at his death. Witness: John LITTLEJOHN, Violinda MUSGROVE, Margaret MUSGROVE. This will or instrument of writing proven by John LITTLEJOHN and ordered certified, 17 October 1783. To entitle Mr. MOXLEY to his brother's pay he must procure a certificate of the time he served in each separate rank in the army. 15 December

1801 Admr with the will annexed granted Wm. MOXLEY, bond and security given.

Bk:Pg: 01:510 [bottom] Date: 10 August 1810

Rec'd. of C. BINNS a deed made by Saml. CLAPHAM to me, for 120¾a in Loudoun bearing date 28 April 1810. Signed Edward MARLOW, 10 August 1810.

Bk:Pg: 01:511 – 01:512 Date: 28 February 1829

John J. MATHIAS of Loudoun to heirs of the late William HAWLING dec'd of Loudoun. Release of trust on 201a. William HAWLING dec'd on 26 October 1821 executed to MATHIAS a trust deed to secure payment of bonds or notes therein set forth to Samuel CLAPHAM (Deed Book 3D, page 177). Trustees of Samuel CLAPHAM authorize release. Signed Rich'd. H. HENDERSON.

Bk:Pg: 01:513 – 01:515 Date: 4 November 1829

Samuel MARKS of Loudoun of 1st part, Samuel B. T. CALDWELL of Loudoun of 2nd part and Joshua OSBURN of Loudoun of 3rd part. Trust for debt to OSBURN and to OSBURN as trustee for Margaret HUMPHREY wife of Marcus HUMPHREY using 52¼a nr Blue Ridge Mt. part of tract formerly belonging to Abel MARKS now deceased, adj Moriss [Morris] OSBURN lately the dower land of the widow of Abel MARKS dec'd, ___ DANIELS, Watts MARKS, Bennet MARKS. Witness: Richard OSBURN, Morris OSBURN, Ann CRAIG.

Bk:Pg: 01:516 – 01:517 Date: 18 December 1822

Thomas MARKS of Loudoun of 1st part, Joshua OSBURN of Loudoun of 2nd part and Margaret HUMPHREY wife of Marcus HUMPHREY of 3rd part. Land formerly the property of Abel MARKS dec'd was assigned to Mary MARKS widow and relict of Abel dec'd as her dower and the reversionary right of Marcus HUMPHREY was by him given up to the Sheriff and by the Sheriff sold to Thomas MARKS. Trust for benefit of Thomas' sister Margaret HUMPHREY. Witness: Bennit MARKS, Lydia MARKS, Abel MARKS. *Proven 8 December 1827 by Lydia MARKS & 10 December 1827 by Abel MARKS.*

Bk:Pg: 01:518 – 01:519 Date: 13 November 1820

Release of trust by John MARKS. Trust dated 10 March 1820 between Saml. SINCLAIR & wife Ruth to Edw'd. B. GRADY, all of Loudoun, using land formerly the property of John MARKS & Stephen McPHERSON Junr. & by them conveyed to SINCLAIR, upon his merchant mill now stands (Deed Book 3A, page 130). GRADY declares his name was only used as trustee for John MARKS of Loudoun. The land was sold by the Sheriff to John

MARKS. Witness: Geo. SWEARINGEN, A. V. POWELL, Lee W. DENHAM.

Bk:Pg: 01:520 – 01:521 Date: 18 June 1819
Patrick B. MEHOLLIN/MILHOLLIN of Loudoun to Sarah MEHOLLIN, Ewell MEHOLLIN and Diademia MEHOLLIN of Loudoun. Gift of lot and houses in Leesburg on Loudoun St. adj Jesse DAILEY, Prince St., Mark WOOD, James GARNER. Acknowledged by Patrick in Jefferson Co. 1 April 1820 before David HUMPHREYS, Rich'd. WILLIAMS.

Bk:Pg: 01:522 – 01:523 Date: 4 November 1826
Robert McINTYRE of 1st part, Eben T. HANCOCK of 2nd part and Ramey G. SAUNDERS of 3rd part, all of Loudoun. Trust for debt to HANCOCK using interest in undivided real estate of Patrick McINTYRE dec'd as one of the heirs. Witness: Josiah L. DREAN, C. C. McINTYRE, L. BEARD.

Bk:Pg: 01:524 – 01:525 Date: 6 September 1817
Patrick B. MEHOLLIN/MILHOLLIN of Loudoun to Boller MEHOLLIN & Patrick MEHOLLIN of Loudoun. Gift of 500a adj John WILLIAMS, Joseph PUSEY, Reubin SCHOOLEY, Richard GRIFFITH, Joseph CALDWELL, JONES & BROWN. Acknowledged by Patrick B. in Jefferson Co. Va 1 March 1820 before David HUMPHREYS, Rich'd. WILLIAMS.

Bk:Pg: 01:526 – 01:528 Date: 26 February 1828
Joseph MOORE of Loudoun to William MERSHON. Trust for forthcoming bonds on suit using 7a where he now lives in occupation of his son James MOORE on Turnpike Road. Chancery suit in name of Mary HOGE, Frederick CRIDER who died & the suit was reinstated in name of his Admr., injunction was dissolved and an execution issued against Jos. MOORE. Witness: Peter SKINNER, John MOORE, Wm. MERSHON.

Bk:Pg: 01:529 Date: 1 February 1814
Abel MARKS of Loudoun to John WHITE. Bill of sale for two negroes named Sook and Ruth. Witness: Silas GLASSCOCK, Thomas WHITE, Mary MARKS. *Proven 1 August 1814 by Thomas WHITE.*

Bk:Pg: 01:530 – 01:531 Date: 2 April 1805
John MARTIN Senr. of Loudoun to Margaret McILHANY widow of James McILHANY dec'd, Nathaniel DAVISON, Lewis ELLZEY, John, Eliza, Mary, Sicelia, James, Luiza and Mortimer McILHANY heirs of James McILHANY dec'd. Assignment of lease for 100a.

George W. FAIRFAX granted lease 1 April 1786 to John MARTIN Senr. Witness: James HAMILTON, John MARTIN Junr., George SHAFFER. *Proven 8 September 1806 by James HAMILTON.*

Bk:Pg: 01:532 – 01:533 Date: 15 March 1781

Charles McMANAMY & wife Jane of Loudoun to James ROACH of Loudoun. Assignment of lease of 150a in lease for lives dated 12 September 1765 from Col. John TAYLOE of Richmond Co. Va to McMANAMY. Witness: J. BLAIR, Robert CHALFANT, John THOMAS. *Proven 10 May 1784 by John THOMAS & Robert CHALFANT.*

Bk:Pg: 01:534 – 01:535 Date: 5 April 1824

John S. MARLOW to Adam WINSEL. Trust for debt to John WINSEL Sr. using 221½a under the Short Hill known as the "Stears farm" purchased of D. DIGGS. Witness: Geo. MARLOW, Thos. J. MARLOW, Hanson MARLOW. *Proven 14 April 1824 by Thomas & Jonathan MARLOW.*

Bk:Pg: 01:536 – 01:539 Date: 11 December 1812

Mary MEGEATH and Stephen MEGEATH & wife Rebekah to Daniel BROWN, all of Loudoun. Bargain and sale of 9a on Beaverdam branch of Goose Creek below paved road leading to Snickers Gap; also one other acre condemned for abuting a dam. Witness: Step. C. ROSZEL, Jacob SMITH, Garret WALKER, Henry ELLIS. Acknowledged by Stephen McGEATH 4 January 1814. Certificate of examination of Rebecca McGEATH returned 29 April 1822 by Burr POWELL, Wm. BRONAUGH, Francis W. LUCKETT.

Bk:Pg: 01:540 Date: 16 September 1778

Valentine MILLER of Shelburn Parish to John Connard SHANKS allis CODY. Trust for debt using farm animals and items. Witness: Robt. JAMISON, two names in foreign language. *Proven 10 May 1779 by Robert JAMISON.*

Bk:Pg: 01:541 Date: 24 September 1814

John MARKS of Loudoun to Benit MARKS of Loudoun. Power of attorney to recover money due. Witness: E. ALLEN, Abel MARKS Seainyear [Senior], Abel MARKS, Junr. *Proven 13 February 1815 by Abel MARKS.*

Bk:Pg: 01:542 – 01:547 Date: 1 June 1784

John Howard MARSHALL of Charles Co. Md to Jacob REED of Loudoun. Bargain and sale of ___ acres. Witness: William COCKE, George FUHOR, John MOORE. *Proven 9 May 1785 by John MOORE.*

Bk:Pg: 01:548 – 01:550 Date: 10 October 1810
John MILLER of Loudoun to Ezekiel CHAMLIN of Loudoun. Bargain and sale of 100a where John now lives (five life lease made by John CARLISLE attorney in fact for George William FAIRFAX to Benjamin DAVIS, by him assigned to Casper QUICK dec'd by deed of assignment, by Casper sold to John PHILIPS, by John to Rhode PHILIPS and by Rhode to Christian MILLER dec'd father to John). Witness: Edward CUNARD, Edward RINCKER, Rich'd. B. HENDERSON. *Proven 11 February 1811 by Edward CUNNARD & Richard HENDERSON.*

Bk:Pg: 01:551 – 01:553 Date: 8 June 1818
William McPHERSON of Loudoun of the 1st part, Cuthbert HARRIS of Fauquier Co. of 2nd part and William HARRIS of Fauquier Co. of 3rd part. Trust for debt to William HARRIS (as security to Benjamin V. LAKIN and others) using household items. Witness: George B. WHITING, Smith DULIN, Benj. V. LAKIN, Edward ELLMORE.

Bk:Pg: 01:554 – 01:556 Date: 15 August 1827
James L. MARTIN of Loudoun to Joseph T. NEWTON of Loudoun. Trust for debt using 11a on south side of Leesburg Turnpike (Lot No. 8 on plat for land sold of late Ricketts & Newton). Witness: James THOMAS, James GILMORE, Saml. HAMMETT.

Bk:Pg: 01:557 – 01:558 Date: 12 June 1772
Harrison MANLEY & wife Margaret sold on 16 June 1772 to John THORNTON 175a in Loudoun. Certificate of examination for Margaret returned 16 June 1772 by John WEST, Sampson DANIEL.

Bk:Pg: 01:558 [bottom] Date: undated
[top part cut off]
WHITE's Admr. vs WHITE – discont.
GARNER vs TAYLOR stone mason – cont'd.
SIM vs McMICKIN – cont'd.
PEAKE vs. ALLEXANDER – cont'd.
SIM vs SAUNDERS – cont'd.
PHILIPS vs BIRKELY – new sums. to pred.
FOWLER vs NIXON – cont'd.
LLOYD vs BOZELL – new sums.
LLOYD vs DAWSON – in schedule, judgm't.

Bk:Pg: 01:559 – 01:561 Date: 8 June 1818
William McPHERSON of Loudoun of 1st part, Cuthbert HARRIS of Fauquier Co. of 2nd part and William HARRIS of Fauquier Co. of 3rd part. Trust for debt to William HARRIS using household items.

Witness: Geo. B. WHITING, Smith DULIN, Benj. V. LAKIN, Edward ELLMORE.

Bk:Pg: 01:562 – 01:563 Date: 4 January 1808
Jonathan McVEIGH of Loudoun to William VICKERS of Loudoun. Assignment of lease of 50a. James LEITH granted lease on 11 April 1801 to McVEIGH for term of 99 years. Witness: Amos JOHNSON, Jesse McVEIGH, Burr POWELL, Thomas WILSON, Hugh ROGERS. *Proven 11 January 1808 by Burr POWELL & Thomas NELSON* [WILSON].

Bk:Pg: 01:563 [bottom] Date: 24 May 1798
From the Clk of Loudoun a deed from Hugh MARTIN ??? to John POTTS which I prom[i]ced to return to the Office. Signed Thos. BACKHOUSE. Witness: Alex'r. WAUGH.

Bk:Pg: 01:564 – 01:567 [top] Date: 2 May 1809
Gabriel McGEATH & wife Patty of Loudoun to Armistead LONG & William BRONAUGH of Loudoun. Trust for debt to John LITTLEJOHN attorney in fact of Michael BELL using 116a adj JACKSON's patent. Witness: Step. C. ROSZEL, Benjamin WALKER, John VANHORN. *Proven 10 April 1810 by John VANHORNE.*

Bk:Pg: 01:567 [bottom] Date: 15 February 1806
John MITCHELL of Loudoun to Thomas YANCEY of Loudoun. Bill of sale for negro woman slave Ann & her two children Henry & Joan Witness: Ludwell LEE, James MITCHELL. *Proven 8 September 1806 by James MITCHELL.*

Bk:Pg: 01:568 Date: 22 May 1826
Samuel MILLER of Fauquier Co. to James McILHANY of Loudoun. Articles of agreement – in 1814 MILLER became purchaser of unimproved lot on Cornwall St. in Leesburg under trust from Bertrand EWELL to Fleet SMITH & Armistead LONG (see Deed Book 2H, page 190). No conveyance was ever received by MILLER. MILLER agrees to transfer to McILHANY his contract under trust. Witness: Jas. H. WOLFE, Joseph CARR.

Bk:Pg: 01:569 – 01:571 Date: 19 August 1812
William McFARLING & wife Rachel of Loudoun to Samuel MOOR of Loudoun. Bargain and sale of 9a adj lands formerly owned by Andrew HESSER dec'd and that of George LEWIS dec'd near the Black Oak Ridge (being ½ of land conveyed by Wm. BURKE to McFARLING and MOOR). Witness: Wm. BRONAUGH, Joshua OSBURN, N. C. WILLIAMS. Certificate of examination for Rachel

returned 19 August 1812 by N. C. WILLIAMS, Joshua OSBURN. *Proven by Joshua OSBOURNE 13 December 1813 & by N. WILLIAMS 14 March 1814.*

Bk:Pg: 01:572 Date: 1 January 1815

Memorandum of agreement entered on 1 January 1815 between Ann MOSS of Loudoun and Vincent MOSS of Loudoun. Ann binds herself to Vincent full and in line percession of the following property: the farm where Ann now lives together with all the survants Jon Benn Ruben Beck and Murr and the stock and farming utencils and grain, and house and furniture and one of the survants Benn or Ruben to drive her carridg whenever & Beck to wate on her whenever she require and her borde and free from all charge and expence except her cloathing and Vincent obliges himself to pay Ann $150 each and every year. Witness: Jacob DAYMUD, William DAYMUDE. *Proven 12 August 1816 by William DAYMUDE.*

Bk:Pg: 01:573 Date: 2 April 1824

James McCRAY of 1st part, Daniel VERNON of 2nd part and Rachel DANIEL of 3rd part. Trust for debt to DANIEL using 1¾a on north side of Goose Creek (conveyed by Alfred CLEMENS & wife to David CARTER and from CARTER to McCRAY). Also signed by Mary McCRAY. Witness: John KEENE, A. B. McMULLIN, Thomas LEONARD.

Bk:Pg: 01:574 – 01:577 Date: 10 April 1819

Andrew McMULLIN & wife Nancy of Loudoun to John MOUNT of Loudoun. Bargain and sale of 102a. Alexander McMULLIN dec'd by his will bequeath to his three sons (William, Daniel and Andrew) 300a on Beaverdam branch of Goose Creek equally divided. The sons on the 15th of April 1812 with the assistance of John SINCLAIR surveyor proceeded to divide per agreement. Certificate of examination for Nancy returned 10 April 1819 by Thos. GREGG, Wm. BRONAUGH.

Bk:Pg: 01:578 Date: 23 April 179_

John MOOR/MOORE to Jacob ISH. Memorandum of agreement – bargain and sale of 2a to be taken from his plantation adj Joseph LACEY, Turnpike Road with use of the stream. Witness: David CARLILE, John BARNET. *Proven 11 February 1793 by David CARLISLE.*

Bk:Pg: 01:579 – 01:580 Date: 23 March 1826

John J. MATHIAS & George RICHARD of Loudoun to John ALT of Loudoun. Release of trust on Lot No. 5 to John ALT & wife Polly dated 20 December 1824 to secure debt (Deed Book 3I, page 192) using 76a (Lots No. 1, No. 2 & No.5 in Wm. ALT's estate). Witness: Saml. M. EDWARDS, Alfred A. ESKRIDGE, Robordeau ANNIN, William J. JONES, William THRIFT.

Bk:Pg: 01:581 – 01:586 Date: 4 March 1822

Nathaniel MANNING & wife Uphamia, Thomas GRIGGS & wife Castalina and William PAXTON & wife Didamia of Loudoun to Jesse RICE & wife Thurza of Loudoun. Bargain and sale of 150a adj RICE, MAINS, VANDEVANTER, WILLIAMS, BINNS. Superior Ct. of Chancery at Winchester on 28 November 1821 in suit of RICE against Reuben SCHOOLEY and Thomas PHILIPS Exors. of David LACEY dec'd, Nathaniel MANNING & wife Uphamia, Thomas GRIGGS & wife Castalina, William PAXTON & wife Didamia and Sarah LACEY, ordered that defendants convey 150a in the bill to RICE. [no witnesses]

Bk:Pg: 01:578 – 01:588 Date: 11 March 1820

James McBRIDE of Loudoun to Ferdinando FAIRFAX of Fairfax Co. Mortgage of 50a at foot of Blue Ridge Mt. in Loudoun (deed of 2 September 1819 FAIRFAX conveyed to McBRIDE). Witness: William HICKMAN, George MILLER, Ebenezer GRUBB, William BLINCOE. *Proven 23 June 1821 by William HICKMAN.*

Bk:Pg: 01:589 Date: 18 March 1816

James McGAHEY & wife Nancy and Samuel HARDY of Loudoun to David McGAHEY of Loudoun. Bargain and sale of undivided shares of land conveyed to George HARDY now dec'd by Isaac LAROWE being the part conveyed to LAROWE by Henry McCABE. Witness: Brumfieald LONG, Jacob COORE?, Isaac LAROWE. *Proven 14 October 1816 by I. LAROWE & B. LONG.*

Bk:Pg: 01:590 – 01:592 Date: 20 February 1825

William M. McCARTY of Loudoun to Lewis A. BEATTY of Frederick Co. Maryland. Memorandum of agreement - McCARTY has rented his farm on the Potomac on the lower side of river being in Loudoun for term of 10 years commensing at this date. Witness: Alfred A. ESKRIDGE, William CLINE, W. J. KING [very difficult to read handwriting]

Bk:Pg: 01:593 Date: 1 October 1807

Thomas McCOWAT of Leesburg to Helen CURTIS of Leesburg. Release of claim on lot at King & Market Sts. in Leesburg. Witness: John MINES, Joseph KNOX, John McCORMICK. *Proven 28 May 1825 by Joseph KNOX & Jonathan McCORMICK.*

Bk:Pg: 01:594 – 01:595 Date: 16 November 1809
Matthew MITCHELL and Reuben SCHOOLEY of Loudoun to Wilson C. SELDEN of Loudoun. Trust for debt to Thomas SWANN using lot on Loudoun St. in Leesburg conveyed by Stephen DONALDSON & wife Susannah to MITCHELL and SCHOOLEY on 13 November 1809. Witness: John LITTLEJOHN, George HEAD, S. BLINCOE, Wil[l]iam SCHOOOLEY {sic}. *Proven 13 March 1810 by John LITTLEJOHN & Sampson BLINCOE.*

Bk:Pg: 01:596 – 01:597 Date: 23 March 1835
Jonathan EWERS of Loudoun to Stephen McPHERSON (of William) & wife Cecelia of Loudoun. Release of trust using 135a adj Benjamin STRINGFELLOW dated 23 Jul 1831 (Deed Book 3W, page 235). Witness: Seth SMITH, Thos. FARELL [or FARED/FRED], Thos. EWERS.

Bk:Pg: 01:598 – 01:599 Date: 1 June 1849
John MOSS of Loudoun to Thomas SAUNDERS Sheriff of Loudoun. MOSS in custody on a capias ad satisfaciendum. Bargain and sale (by act for relief of insolvent debtors) of interest in 101a where MOSS now resides adj Isaac CARR, Ignatius ELGIN. [no witness signatures]

Bk:Pg: 01:600 – 01:601 Date: 30 March 1850
Mahlon McCARTOR of Loudoun to S. B. T. CALDWELL of Loudoun. Bill of sale for ½ of crop as per article of agreement, also my 1/3 share in wheat growing on my land and seeded by Benj'n. OGDEN. Witness: Geo. W. CALDWELL, Charles C. CALDWELL.

Bk:Pg: 01:602 – 01:603 Date: 15 September 1847
Hiram McVEIGH to ___ High Sheriff of Loudoun. McVEIGH in custody of Sheriff of Frederick Co. Va by a capias de satisfaciendum. Bargain and sale (as act of insolvent debtor) of house & 3/8a lot in Hillsborough, also lot with stable purchased of heirs of Thomas HOUGH dec'd adj same, also a 15a lot on the east side of Short Hill near Hillsborough purchased of James & Mathew McILHANY, also 641a tract in Monroe (now Audrain) in Missouri purchased of Geo. L. COCHRAN subject to trust. [no witness signatures]

Bk:Pg: 01:604 Date: __ December 1831
Athcenath McKIM to uncle William WRIGHT. Bargain and sale of interest in both real and personal estate of dec'd grandfather Patison WRIGHT. Witness: __ DULANEY, J. T. GRIFFITH, Edward THOMPSON.

Bk:Pg: 01:605 – 01:606 Date: 3 October 1822

James McBRIDE & wife Mary of Loudoun to Thomas KIDWELL. Bargain and sale of 50a on east side of Blue Ridge adj Ebenezer GRUBB, ___ MILTON. Witness: George GARNER, Jacob SHRIVER, Antony STULL, John STIDMAN. *Proven 4 November 1826 by Jonathan STEADMAN.*

Bk:Pg: 01:607 Date: 17 Feb [torn]

Charles STEWART and John DOWDELL to Thomas NEALE. Assignment of lease on 120a (from Jeremiah COCKRILL attorney in fact for William L [torn]) adj Richard NEALE, Horsepen branch. Witness: George NEALE, Moses PILCHER, Jno. HUTCHISON Junr. *Proven 9 May 1803 by George NEALE & John HUTCHISON.*

Bk:Pg: 01:608 – 01:609 Date: 18 June 1806

John NICKLIN (formerly John NICKLIN Junr.) of Monongalia Va to Jonathan CUNNARD of Loudoun. Release of trust to John NICKLIN Senr. (now dec'd) made 7 May 1804 using 50¾a CUNNARD purchased of John NICKLIN Junr. Witness: James HAMILTON, N. DAVISSON, Isaac HOUGH, Wm. YOE. *Proven 9 September 1804 by Isaac HOUGH & Nathaniel DAVISSON.*

Bk:Pg: 01:610 Date: 20 April 1815

Conn O'NEIL and Silas REASE. Bond for agreement. George NIXON of Loudoun by agreement of 20 April 1815 agreed to give up claim to all the property he obtained by intermarriage with his present wife Mary formerly Mary FITZSIMONS. Mary relinquishes claim to estate of George. Witness: W. CHILTON, David NIXON, John WILSON, Daniel O. REES.

Bk:Pg: 01:611 – 01:613 Date: 5 December 1812

Ignatious NORRIS & wife Mary of Loudoun of 1st part to John KIPHEART of Loudoun of 2nd part and John PAYNE of 3rd part. Trust for debt using one moiety or ½ of lot on north side of Cornwell St. in Leesburg being the easternmost ½ of ½a Lot No. 42; adj William TAYLOR, Frederick DRISH. Lot was formerly the property of Benjamin HUFTY now Captain John ROSE. Witness: S. BLINCOE, John PAYNE, J. MOFFETT Junior. *Proven 11 August 1813 by S. BLINCOE.*

Bk:Pg: 01:614 – 01:616 Date: 4 November 1806

Joseph T. NEWTON of Loudoun to William NEWTON of Alexandria, District of Columbia. Bargain and sale of one moiety or ½ of two undivided tracts of land - 143a purchased of Samuel D. HARRIMAN and conveyed by Benjamin EDWARDS of Thomas Laswell LEE and the balance of HARRIMAN and conveyed by EDWARDS to Enoch

FRANCIS and by FRANCIS to Joseph T. NEWTON) adjoining to each other on east side of Goose Creek, adj. ___ EDWARDS, Samuel D. HARRIMAN bought of John WREN; and 61a (Enoch FRANCIS purchase of Peter HARBOURT and conveyed one moiety to Joseph T. NEWTON and one moiety of the toll bridge conveyed by FRANCIS) adj Goose Creek. Witness: Isaac LAROWE, Enoch FRANCIS, Thos. BOLTON. *Proven 8 December 1806 by Isaac LAROWE & 14 September 1807 by Thomas BOLTON.*

Bk:Pg: 01:617 – 01:619 Date: 8 May 1814

Henry NEER and David NEER [rest of document gives as Amos] of Loudoun to Thomas SWAN of Alexandria and Enoch MASON of Stafford Co. Va. Trust for debt of Henry NEER and Amos NEER to William Dudley DIGGES of Prince Georges Co. Md their four separate obligations date 23 December 1814 using 110a generally known as William Dudley DIGGES short hill tract [purchased from DIGGES & wife Elleenorah 23 December 1814], adj __ NEISWANGER, David NEER. Witness: David NEER, William DERRY, George SMITH, Jno. MATHIAS, John MOORE.

Bk:Pg: 01:620 Date: 25 Jul 1789

Anne NEALE Admx. of Thos. NEALE dec'd to George CURTIS. Bill of sale of Negroe Bob aged about 12y. Witness: Hugh TALBUTT, Hector R. ESKRIDGE. *Proven 14 September 1789 by Hugh TALBERT.*

Bk:Pg: 01:621 – 01:622 Date: 10 September 1817

Samuel & Isaac NICHOLS of Loudoun to John WRIGHT of Loudoun. Release of trust of 30 March 1809 using 25a. Witness: James BRANDON, Phebe NICHOLS.10 November 1817 ackn'd. by S. NICKOLLS.

Bk:Pg: 01:623 – 01:625 Date: 17 November 1819

Bazil NEWMAN of Loudoun to Silas WHERRY of Loudoun. Trust for debt to William AULT/ALT using 20a conveyed this day by AULT. Witness: Jno. J. MATHIAS, Lee W. DENHAM, Geo. SWEARINGEN.

Bk:Pg: 01:626 Date: 20 April 1815

George NIXON of Loudoun to Conn O'NEIL and Silas REECE of Loudoun. All property of his wife Mary NIXON formerly Mary FITZSIMONS before their marriage put in trust to remain at her disposal. Witness: Wm. CHILTON, David NIXON. *Proven 14 June 1815 by William CHILTON & 9 October 1815 by David NIXON.*

Bk:Pg: 01:627 – 01:630 Date: 14 April 1788

Thomas NEALE of Loudoun to Charles ESKRIDGE of Loudoun. Thomas and wife Ann have been unhappy for some time and have agreed to live apart. Trust for benefit of Ann using 600a in Fairfax and Loudoun on Difficult Run; also Negro woman Nell and girl Nan; and household items and jewels; until Ann dies or they live together again. Witness: Presley Carr LANE, Charles C. JONES, W. BRENT. 9 June 1788 proven by C. Courts JONES & ord'd. cert'd.

Bk:Pg: 01:631 – 01:632 Date: 19 November 1846

Charles B. OBANNON to Cuthbert POWELL Sheriff of Loudoun. Charles now in custody of Sheriff on an execution in name of Elijah HUTCHISON for use of John LAWSON for debt from 1 January 1842. Bargain and sale by act of insolvent debtor using 185a (purchased by OBANNON of heirs of Andrew HUTCHISON) in Loudoun & Fairfax Co. adj Sanford HUTCHISON, Thos. B. MERSHON heirs, Bertrand EWELL. [no witness signatures]

Bk:Pg: 01:633 – 01:634 Date: 15 January 1831

Daniel EATCHES/EACHES trustee and Isaac NICHOLS, William PIGGOTT, William HOGE and Thomas HATCHER Exors. of Samuel and Isaac NICKOLS dec'd of Loudoun to William VICKERS of Loudoun. Release of instrument of writing dated 29 June 1812 for debt. [no witness signatures] Acknowledged by EACHES 19 September 1831.

Bk:Pg: 01:635 Date: 14 Jul 1788

Thomas KING and Timothy HIXON of Shelburne Parish Overseers of the Poor for First Battalion to Charles BINNS Jr. of same. Binds out Letty DALIHAN aged 10y on the 16th of Jan next to BINNS to serve from this date until she arrives to full age of 18 years. Witness: Alex. KING, Jno. BINNS.

Bk:Pg: 01:636 – 01:638 Date: 26 December 1835

Thornton F. OFFUTT of 1st part, Thornton WALKER of 2nd part and Samuel NIXON and James STEPHENSON of 3rd part. Trust for debt to NIXON dated 20 September 1833 as security for debts to Tholemiah and Alfred RHODES, Morris OSBURN, John CABELL, James STEPHENSON using house and lot in Snickersville in occupancy of OFFUTT (conveyed from William CLINE). Witness: Thompson CLAYTON, James M. CLAUGHNEY, G. M. POWELL. 8 August 1836 at 5 o'clock afternoon & ack'd. by WALKER. 10 January 1839 proven by Jas. M. CLAUGHNEY. 16 March 1839 ordered that Clerk of Ct. deliver to NIXON and STEPHENSON a deed of trust.

Bk:Pg: 01:639 – 01:640 Date: 12 April 1758
Settlement account sheet for Ferdinando ONEAL to James Ingo DOZIER beginning 11 November 1755. Find for the Plaintiff 1,224 lbs. crop tob. at £2.1.5 and damages. Signed Thos. LEWISE.

Bk:Pg: 01:641 – 01:643 Date: 26 February 1808
Thomas PHILIPS and William PAXON of Loudoun of 1st part, John McGATH/McGEATH & wife Elizabeth of Loudoun of 2nd part and Anthony CONARD of Loudoun of 3rd part. Release of trust for debt dated 5 June 1806 using 117a. Witness: Jno. MATHIAS, Rich'd. NORWOOD, Wm. WRIGHT, John WILLIAMS, Nathan BALL, Saml. PIERPOINT. *Acknowledged 12 April 1808 by John & Elizabeth McGEATH.*

Bk:Pg: 01:644 – 01:646 Date: 13 March 1795
Franklin PERRY of Loudoun to Isaac HOUGH of Loudoun. Bargain and sale of land adj PERRY, Mrs. Mary BRUSTER; also with free passage to the nighest spring. Witness: John JACKSON Jr., Jno. S. PERRY, Peggy PERRY, J. GILPIN, Thos. EVERIT, Hugh CONN. Receipt of 23 March 1795 witnesses Jno. S. PERRY, John JACKSON Jr., J. GILPIN, Thomas EVERIT, Peggy PERRY, Hugh CONN.

Bk:Pg: 01:647 – 01:651 Date: 12 January 1807
Francis H. PEYTON (heir at law of Dade PEYTON dec'd of Leesburg) & wife Frances of Leesburg to William LITTLEJOHN and John H. CANBY (as tenants in common and not as joint tenants) of Leesburg. Bargain and sale of 1,000a on west fork of Brush Creek in Adam Co. Ohio (being ½ of 2,000a). Witness: Jas. CAVAN Jr., John PAYNE, Thos. WILKINSON. Certificate of examination of 13 January 1807 for Frances returned by Leven LUCKETT, William NOLAND. Certificate of examination for Margaret, wife of Henry PEYTON, Gent. for deed dated 16 November 1771 to Leven POWEL[L], taken 16 December 1771 by Howson HOOE, Wm. ALEXANDER.

Bk:Pg: 01:652 Date: 18 June 1832
Samuel PEUGH of Loudoun to Cyrus BURSON of Loudoun. Release of trust dated 10 November 1826 for trust conveyed to James HOGE using land conveyed to Cyrus by Joseph BURSON & wife Mary. [no witnesses]

Bk:Pg: 01:653 – 01:654 Date: 5 April 1838
Elizabeth PRICE to Thomson F. MASON of Alexandria, District of Columbia of real and personal property per terms of deed. (Deed dated 23 November 1833 from George PRICE & wife to Richard H.

HENDERSON, power granted Elizabeth PRICE to dispose of property in deed.) Witness: Charles GREENWALT, Charles W. GIST, Elizabeth BOYD.

Bk:Pg: 01:655 – 01:656 Date: 15 August 1827
Humph. PEAKE and George WISE, Commissioners acting under a decree of Aug Ct. of Alexandria Co. to James GILMORE of Loudoun. Bargain and sale of 2a on south side of Leesburg Turnpike Road (Lot No. 6 of Ricketts & Newton). Witness: James THOMAS, James F. NEWTON, Rich'd. H. LOVE.

Bk:Pg: 01:657 – 01:658 Date: 23 January 1841
George W. PAINTER of Loudoun to Jesse PORTER of Loudoun. Trust for debt to Peter DERRY using all his personal property. [no witness signatures] 25 January 1841 acknowledged by PAINTER.

Bk:Pg: 01:659 – 01:660 Date: 15 October 1832
Scott Co., Kentucky. Clerk certifies that Job STEVENSON and John BRANHAM, Gentlemen had a power of attorney from Bailey PAYNE & others to Alfred OFFUTT acknowledged by Bailey PAYNE, Rebecca JAMES, Jacob MILLER, Garland JOHNSON and Bailey PAYNE as Guardian for Sanford DEHAVEN. Certificate of examination for Sally PAYNE the wife of Bailey PAYNE, Nancy MILLER wife of Jacob MILLER, Therisa JOHNSON wife of Garland JOHNSON.

Bk:Pg: 01:661 – 01:664 Date: 7 June 1832
Settlement acct. Sorry to have left home just two days before the date of your favor of the 19th cur't. for the Superior Court at Winchester wherein I did not return until today. I found here administered upon the estate of Amos SINCLAIR dec'd and sold his land as a commissioner of the court. At the time I last wrote you I was under a mistaken impression as to the amount due to Benj'n. SINCLAIR not knowing that he was only a half brother of Amos SINCLAIR dec'd. There were two of the half and eight of the whole blood and I should have given the half blood only half as much as the whole blood. It is thus B. SINCLAIR's interest I sent down as per my statement. The amount of the personal estate is what is left of the payment of debts & expenses, the share of the first payment for the land is less than those of the second and third because the entire expenses of the sale including the amount [creased] taken out of the first pay't. I charge ten dollars in settling the business and receiving and paying the money leaving due ninety six dollars 34/100 for which I send you a check noted good by the cashier of the bank here for which W. B. SMITH Cash'r of the U. S. Bank will give you the

cash. Signed Rich'd. H. HENDERSON Written on side * There were 8 whole & two half bloods. Signed A. D. OFFUTT.

2 October 1832 - Whereas Amos SINCLAIR of Loudoun departed without children leaving the following heirs at law: Bailey PAYNE & wife Sarah late Sarah DEHAVEN, Rebekka JAMES late Rebekka DEHAVEN, Jacob MILLER & wife Nancy late Nancy DEHAVEN, Garland JOHNSON & wife Thursa late Thursa DEHAVEN and Sanford DEHAVEN by his Guardian Bailey PAYNE, the two last the children of Nelly DEHAVEN by Bailey PAYNE & all of them the children of Polly DEHAVEN dec'd late Polly SINCLAIR. They appoint their friend Alfred OFFUTT to transact business with said estate. Witness: John SUTPHIN, Matthew BERKLEY.

Bk:Pg: 01:665 – 01:666 Date: 24 April 1779

Isaac HUMPHREY of Loudoun to Thomas HUMPHREY of Loudoun. Lease for one year of 227a granted Isaac HUMPHREY from proprietors office of Northern Neck of Va 21 June 1777 adj Hannah BROOKS, Leven POWELL. [no witness signatures] *Proven 14 June 1779 by Benjamin BARTON & 11 October 1779 by Sam BUTCHER.*

Bk:Pg: 01:667 – 01:669 Date: 29 Jul 1819

John HAMMAT & wife Frances, Samuel HAMMAT & wife Winifred, Giles HAMMAT, George HAMMAT, Lindsey THOMAS & wife Nancy heirs and representatives of George HAMMAT dec'd of Loudoun to Edward HAMMAT. Bargain and sale of 4a devised by Geo. HAMMAT dec'd to James HAMMAT subject to the life estate of Sarah HAMMAT, on north side of road leading from Leesburg to WILLIAMS smith shop (Deed Book K, page 283). [no witness signatures] Certificate of examination for Nancy THOMAS dated 23 June 1821 returned by Samuel MURREY, Presley CORDELL Senr. *Acknowledged 29 Jul 1819 by Giles & George HAMMETT and 18 June 1821 by Samuel HAMMAT & Lindsey THOMAS.*

Bk:Pg: 01:670 Date: 8 March 1810

Susannah HOUSHOLDER Admx. of estate of Adam HOUSHOLDER dec'd, Adam HOUSHOLDER and David AXLINE to Daniel HOUSHOLDER. Relinquishment all claim to a lease on a tract whereon Daniel now lives; also the advancement of $200 by his father in his life, doth hereby relinquish to Susannah, Adam and David and the other legatees to the estate of Adam HOUSHOLDER dec'd all his interest in his father's estate. Witness: John HAMILTON, R. BRADEN, Edmund JENINGS, Michael RICKARD.

Bk:Pg: 01:671 – 01:672 Date: 24 February 1829
Elizabeth HUGHES of Homes Co. Ohio to Anna GOODIN of Loudoun. Bargain and sale of undivided interest (of her father Jasper POULSON's estate) in her mother Agnes POULSON's dower at her death; also 13a Lot No. 5 in division of land. Witness: Stacy TAYLOR, Jonathan HEATON, John BIRDSALL, Absalom BEANS. *Proven 10 August 1829 by Jno. GOODIN & Abraham* [Absolom?] *BEANS.*

Bk:Pg: 01:673 – 01:675 Date: 24 August 1813
Christian/Cristian ISH of Bedford Co. Pa to Rezin SPATES of Montgomery Co. Md. Power of attorney to recover debt from Charles DRISH of Loudoun and for sale of interest on land whereon his mother Catherine ISH last resided previous to her going to reside in Leesburgh. Witness: Beal HOWARD, Geo. HOFFMAN. Acknowledged by ISH and proven by witness HOFFMAN in Allegany Co. Md 24 August 1813.

Bk:Pg: 01:676 – 01:678 Date: 11 March 1813
Christian ISH of Pa (by attorney Rezin SPATES), Peter ISH of Loudoun, Charles DRISH & wife Susannah and William JOHNSON & wife Margaret of Loudoun to William NEWTON of Alexandria, District of Columbia. Bargain and sale of interest 75a which was sold by Patrick CAVAN an agent of William WILSON to Catherine ISH now dec'd (died intestate, descended to Christian, Peter, Susannah and Margaret her children and only heirs at law). Witness: William D. DRISH Jr., Nathaniel TRIPLETT, John HAMMERLY, Tho. SWANN, William ELGIN, Tho. R. MOTT, Saml. M. EDWARDS.

Bk:Pg: 01:679 – 01:680 Date: 4 September 1801 [written over]
Peter HICKMAN & wife Regina, Jacob HICKMAN, Elizabeth HICKMAN, Peter SMOUSE & wife Catherine, John WOLF & wife Abigail, John INGLEBREAK & wife Charity (Peter, Jacob, Elizabeth, Catherine, Abigail and Charity the heirs and children of Conrod HICKMAN dec'd who died intestate) of Loudoun to Adam HOUSHOLDER Junior of Loudoun. Bargain and sale of 103a which was conveyed to Conrod HICKMAN now dec'd by Charles Earl of Tankerville and Henry Astley BENNETT on 14 March 1796 (Deed Book X. page 200). Witness: Frederick SMITH, [foreign name], Lawrence MINK, [foreign name].

Bk:Pg: 01:681 Date: 11 November 1775
Anthony RUSSELL, Gent. of Loudoun to Andrew RUSSELL of Loudoun. Bargain and sale of 200a to be laid off including the plantation he now lives on. [no signature or witnesses]

Bk:Pg: 01:682 – 01:683 Date: 14 November 1807
William MANN and Charles Fenton MERCER Commissioners of the U.S. Court, 5th Circuit Va District acting by order at suit of Richard CHESTER and William MASTERMAN Exors. of Daniel MILDRED dec'd (who was surviving partner of MILDRED and ROBERTS, against Samuel HOUGH and others) to Thomas SWANN of Alexandria, District of Columbia. Bargain and sale 223a and mortgage from Samuel and Mahlon HOUGH to Richard CHESTER and William MASTERMAN dated 2 December 1802, on Tuskarora adj ___ CHANDLER, William MAINE's patent, ___ KIMMINS. Witness: William CHILTON, Isaac LAROWE, Jno. MATHIAS, Eli OFFUTT.

Bk:Pg: 01:684 – 01:687 Date: 20 December 1823
Abraham FOULTON/FULTON of Loudoun of 1st part, William NOLAND of Loudoun of 2nd part, and Thomas J. NOLAND of Loudoun of 3rd part. Trust for debt to William using Lots 113 & 114 in Aldie on Mercer Street. Witness: Peter SKINNER, Danl. P. CONRAD, Thos. ROBINSON. *Acknowledged 9 February 1824 by Wm. NOLAND & proven by D. P. CONRAD & Peter SKINNER as to FOULTON.*

Bk:Pg: 01:688 Date: 1 December 1807
Peter ANSELL of Summerset Co. in Turkeyfoot township in Pa to friend and brother Leonard ANSWELL [ANSELL] of Loudoun. Power of attorney to convey his part of plantation of Leonard ANSWELL [ANSELL] dec'd of Loudoun and to receive money and debts. Witness: Timothy HIXSON, Martin ANSEL, Saml. CLAPHAM, William NOLAND. *Proven 8 January 1810 by Timothy HIXON.*

Bk:Pg: 01:689 – 01:690 Date: 9 April 1805
Thomas Ludwell LEE of Loudoun and Landon CARTER, Esqr. of Richmond Co. Va Exors. of George CARTER Esqr. late of Stafford Co. dec'd to Josiah MOFFETT of Loudoun. Bargain and sale of 40a adj Nich's. GARRETT, ___ DEWELL. Witness: John LITTLEJOHN, John McCORMICK, Steph'n COOKE, Jno. MATHIAS. *Proven 10 April 1805 by John McCORMICK & John MATHIAS.*

Bk:Pg: 01:691 Date: __ February 1790
HOLMES to CLAGGETT. Power of Attorney. Ordered that it be certified that it is proven in this Court by Sarah HOLMES widow of Edward HOLMES dec'd that her husband born at Swartmore in Lancashire County England and afterwards removed to Virginia and settled in Loudoun about 1775, that he was brother to William HOLMES late of Loudoun dec'd, that William and Edward HOLMES were sons of Joseph HOLMES and his wife Margaret who was sister

of Edward FELL formerly of Baltimore town in Maryland trader but last of the City of London where he died. Within power of attorney proven by Wm. CRAIG, Joseph JAMES (a Quaker) and Sarah HOLMES widow of Edward HOLMES dec'd. Ord'd to be cert'd. February 1790.

Bk:Pg: 01:692 – 01:693 Date: 3 September 1805

John SPENCER & wife Phebey of Wood Co. Va to Nathenael POLEN of Loudoun. Bargain and sale of 109a (from 238a granted him by Commonwealth on 12 August 1794, Deed Book W, page 536) on south fork of Broad Run of Potomack River, road leading from gum spring meet house to mountain meeting house, adj John HUPP/HOUPP, Israel LACEY. Witness: Andrew REDMOND, Benj. REDMOND, Benjamin GARNER. 9 September 1805 proven by Andrew and Benj. REDMOND.

Bk:Pg: 01:694 – 01:695 Date: 11 August 1788

John SPENCER of Loudoun to Stout BENNETT of Loudoun. Lease for term of 21 years from 1 January 1787 of 67a on south side of Broad Run adj ___ CURTIS, ___ RALL. Jos. LEWIS, John SHEKELL, Banabas [Barnabas] CURTIS. *Proven 8 December 1788 by Joseph LEWIS & Barnabas CURTIS.*

Bk:Pg: 01:696 – 01:697 Date: 11 August 1788

John SPENCER of Loudoun to Barnabas CURTIS of Loudoun. Lease for term of 21 years from 1 Jan '85 of 60a on south side of Broad Run. Witness: John SHEKELL, Jos. LEWIS, Stout BENNETT. *Proven 8 December 1788 by John* [Jos.?] *LEWIS & Stout BENNETT.*

Bk:Pg: 01:698 Date: 30 Au[g] 1795

Intention and desire of John SMARR by his last will and testament to give his daughter Jane the same and equal share with all his children by his first wife and whereas we are conscious that in the visiduary claim of John's will he has by mistake omitted to name his daughter Jane. We agree that she shall have an equal share of his estate with all the children by his first wife. Signed Robt. SMARR, John HAMPTON, Mary HAMPTON, Jesse WILLIAMSON, Nancy WILLIAMSON and Sarah SMARR. Witness: Joseph HAMPTON, Saml. HAMPTON, John PRITCHARD, Wm. BRONAUGH Jr., Francis HUNE Junor, Richard WEADON.

Bk:Pg: 01:699 [top] Date: 5 August 1799

Sarah SMARR of Loudoun (widow of John SMARR dec'd) to daughter Fanny SMARR. Gift of young negroe girl Lett (daughter of Winny). Witness: C. BINNS Jr., Simon BINNS.

Bk:Pg: 01:699 [bottom] Date: 23 March 1808
Rec'd. of Charles BINNS Clerk of Loudoun two deeds from John SPENCER & Phebe his wife to me for 150a each of land lying in Wood Co. proven only by James SPENCER one of the witnesses. Signed Benjamin JAMES. Witness: Isaac LAROWE, Saml. M. EDWARDS, Eli OFFUTT.

Bk:Pg: 01:700 [top] Date: 5 August 1799
Sarah SMARR of Loudoun (widow of John SMARR dec'd) to son Thomas SMARR. Gift of negro boy called Dennis (son of Winny). Witness: C. BINNS Jr., Simon BINNS. *Proven 16 August 1799 by Charles BINNS Jr.*

Bk:Pg: 01:700 [bottom] Date: 12 February 1810
Presley SANDERS Junr. and Henry SANDERS both of Loudoun to John DULIN of Loudoun. Bond – John SANDERS this day executed a deed to John DULIN for 155a. If it shall appear thereafter that there is no incumbrance on said tract and that DULIN can hold the tract free from all manner of incumbrance or claims. Witness: Jno. MATHIAS, Aaron SANDERS. *Proven 14 November 1810 by John MATTHIAS.*

Bk:Pg: 01:701 Date: 14 January 1802
Certificate of examination of Hannah wife of Joshua SINGLETON for partition to the representatives of William RUST dec'd on 422a. Returned 14 January 1802 by Jos. LANE, Ben. GRAYSON.

Bk:Pg: 01:702 Date: 9 January 1813
Wm. M. LITTLEJOHN of Loudoun to John SPOONER a free black man, aged 21y of Loudoun. In consideration of $100 (1/3 paid annually) agrees to faithfully serve & obey LITTLEJOHN for term of three years and provide sufficient food & clothing. Witness: John LITTLEJOHN, John H. LITTLEJOHN Junr. *Proven 12 January 1813 by John LITTLEJOHN.*

Bk:Pg: 01:703 – 01:705 Date: 19 October 1801
David SPENCER & wife Mary of Loudoun to Benjamin JAMES of Loudoun. Bargain and sale of 82a (part of land that John SPENCER now lives on where John MILTON now lives) adj the part that said SPENCER sold to Thomas COCKRIL now belonging to William SMAWLEY, broad run, road from mountain to gum spring. Witness: And'w REDMOND, Francis GULICK, John SPENCER Jur. *Proven 12 April 1802 by Andrew REDMAN & 10 May 1802 by Francis GULICK.*

Bk:Pg: 01:706 Date: 30 November 1808

Lige STILLER to daughter Elizabeth STILLER. Gift of cow and hog. Witness: William CARR, David CARR.

Bk:Pg: 01:707 – 01:708 Date: 21 September 1803

Isaac SIDDELL of Loudoun to James McILHANY of Loudoun. Assignment of lease of 172a during the residue of the term unexpired (George Wm. FAIRFAX by lease of 14 May 1764 granted Moses CADWALADER. On 12 November 1770 CADWALADER assigned to Isaac SIDDLE). Witness: Abner WILLIAMS, John HOUGH, John McILHANY, Mahlon MORRIS, Lewis ELLZEY, Robert MORRIS. *Proven 8 September 1806 by Lewis ELLZEY.*

Bk:Pg: 01:709 – 01:710 Date: __ February 1770

Certificate of examination for Karen Habock wife of Robert SANDFORD for lease/release dated 6 and 7 February 1770 to William Carr LANE, Gent. Returned 7 February 1770 by Jas. LANE, G. SUMMERS.

Bk:Pg: 01:711 – 01:712 Date: __ January 1811

Isaac STEERE Junr. & wife Rebekah of Loudoun to Thomas STEERE of Loudoun. Bargain and sale of 1/3 part of 250a in Harrison Co. purchased by Joseph STEERE now dec'd of James COCKEREL & wife Temperance by conveyance dated 18 January 1802. Witness: William BROWN.

Bk:Pg: 01:713 – 01:714 Date: 12 May 1810

Andrew SMARR of Loudoun to Burr POWELL of Loudoun. Trust for debt to Thomas A. HEREFORD of Loudoun using lot in Middleburg conveyed by Col. Leven POWELL to HEREFORD and conveyed today to SMARR. Witness: Joseph PATTERSON, Tho. P. HEREFORD, Peter MYERS. Paper by Thos. A. HEREFORD assigns his interest in the within deed to John LOVE for value of him received the 12th of May 1810 with same witnesses as before. 12 November 1810 ack'd. by A. SMARR & ord. certif'd.

Bk:Pg: 01:715 Date: 26 February 1821

Elizabeth SPATES late Elizabeth McCABE widow of and Admx. of William McCABE (alias Wm. BLINSTON) dec'd and John T. McCABE son and heir of said Wm. McCABE dec'd to Saml. M. EDWARDS, all of Loudoun. Assignment of 1a that was leased to Wm. McCABE alias Wm. BLINSTON by James HEREFORD (Lease for lives to Wm. McCABE alias BLINSTON, Elizabeth his wife, and John T. his son, dated 13 March 1801, Deed Book 2L, page 425) with liberty of egress and regress to the Spring (commonly called the

Rock Spring). Witness: Thomas SANDERS, P. SAUNDERS, Edw'd HAMMATT. *Proven 25 March 1822 by Edward HAMMATT.*

Bk:Pg: 01:716 0 01:717 Date: 13 September 1826
Lewis M. SMITH of Loudoun to William NOLAND of Independence, territory of Arkansas. Bargain and sale of 2a (Edward HAZEL & wife Elizabeth on 29 March 1822 conveyed to SMITH as trustee 2a on north side of Ashbys turnpike road near Aldie). Witness: Thos. ROBINSON, William HAGERMAN, William F. ADAM. *Proven 13 October 1826 by Thos. ROBINSON.*

Bk:Pg: 01:718 Date: 6 December 1820
Susannah SETTLE of Loudoun to Reuben SETTLE, James SETTLE and John SETTLE of Loudoun. Gift of household items, farm items, horse. Signed by Geo. B. WHITING at request and in presence of Susannah. Witness: Geo. B. WHITING, R. H. LITTLE. *Proven 12 February 1821 by George B. WHITING.*

Bk:Pg: 01:719 – 01:721 [top] Date: 1 Jul 1830
George RICHARDS of 1st part, John SHAW of 2nd part and Simon SMALE of 3rd part. Release of trust of 2 October 1826 using lot in Leesburg on Back St. [no witness signatures] Wm. D. DRISH assignee of Simon SMALE released 3 Jul 1830.

Bk:Pg: 01:721 [bottom] – 01:723 Date: 16 May 1811
Robert SANFORD of Loudoun to James MOORE & John WILLIAMS of Loudoun. Trust for debt to James RATTIKIN of Tuscarawa Co. Ohio using 165a adj RATTIKIN, ___ SCHOOLEY, ___ COX, James NIXSON. Witness: Abner WILLIAMS, W. S. NEALE, William DOUGLASS, William SCHOOLEY. *Proven 11 November 1811 by Abner WILLIAMS.*

Bk:Pg: 01:724 – 01:725 Date: 14 May 1814
Winifred SMITH & Charles SMITH of Loudoun to Ann SMITH (daughter of Charles and granddaughter of Winifred). Gift of negroe woman Sylvia and her child Delpha. Witness: S'n. BLINCOE, Philip COE, Robert COE, David J. COE. Proven 16 May 1816 by S. BLINCOE.

Bk:Pg: 01:726 Date: 10 December 1800
Andrew SMALLEY to brother William SMALLEY of Loudoun. Power of attorney to sell title to 1/6 part of ¼a in Centreville (undivided moiety from estate of Ezek'l. SMALLEY dec'd). Witness: Thos. COCKERILL, John LEWIS of Joseph.

Bk:Pg: 01:727 – 01:729 Date: 11 March 1822
Reuben SCHOOLEY of Loudoun to John MATHIAS of Loudoun. Trust for debt to William SMITH and Archibald MAINS using 6a in west addition of Leesburg adj Martin KITZMILLER, James RUST, Loudoun St. (purchased of John LITTLEJOHN). [no witness signatures] *Proven 11 March 1822 by H. SCHOOLEY.*

Bk:Pg: 01:730 – 01:732 Date: 24 February 1803
John G. STEACKLER of Frederick Co. Md to George ABEL of Loudoun. Assignment of lease of 100a (George William FAIRFAX on 12 September 1765 granted lease for lives to John ROLER (Joseph HOUGH and Simon SHOEMAKER) adj Philip FEEL. ROLER in his will devised land to be sold by Christopher BURNHOUSE and Matthias SMIDLEY his Exors., which they did on 21 [torn off] 1803 to John STEACKLER). Witness: Jacob WYATT, Jacob POTTENFIELD, Benjamin MOORE, George BURNHOUSE, Halling SMITLY. 25 February 1803 receipt for payment signed by BURNHOUSE and SMITLY. Witness: Wm. H. HARDING, Levi HOLE.

Bk:Pg: 01:733 – 01:734 Date: __ February 1803
Benjamin SANDERS and James SANDERS to Lewis MASSEY. Lease of 6a. Witness: Levi HOLE, John TOBIT, David BEALE. *Proven 14 February 1803 by John TOBIT & David BEACH* [BEALE]

Bk:Pg: 01:735 – 01:736 Date: 18 January 1809
John SCHOOLEY Jr. of Loudoun to Thomas JANNEY of Alexandria. Bill of sale for colt. Witness: Daniel GANTT, Fleet SMITH.

Bk:Pg: 01:737 – 01:738 Date: ___ 1808
Aaron SANDERS and Sampson BLINCOE of Loudoun to Leonard ANSILL of Loudoun. Release of trust dated 23 April 1807 to Leonard & wife Susanna using all the share of Henry M. DAVIS & wife Catharine to lands left by Leonard ANSILL dec'd purchased by Leonard in trust for said DAVIS and also the share of Leonard to lands left by his father Leonard ANSILL dec'd. Witness: Fleet SMITH, Eli OFFUTT, Isaac LAROWE. Apr Ct. 1808 ordered to be certified to Montgomery County. Certified accordingly & delivered Wm. CARR. Signed Saml. M. EDWARDS October 1808.

Bk:Pg: 01:739 – 01:742 Date: 20 March 1778
William SANDERS, planter, & wife Rachel of Loudoun to Nehemiah DAVIS, planter of Fairfax Co. Va. Lease for one year of 100a now in possession of DAVIS, adj Thomas LEE Esqr., ___ ASHTON. Witness: Har. LANE, Will. LANE, Alex'r. C. MOTT, Wm. HEADON, Geo. SUMMERS, Scarlitt BERKLEY. 14 September 1778 this

indenture and the rec't endorsed were proven by G. SUMMERS & Har. LANE, Gent.

Bk:Pg: 01:743 Date: 11 June 1783

Robt. STEPHENS, Thomas BEATY and Edwin FURR of Loudoun to William LANE Junior of Loudoun. Bond – Nicholas MINOR & Joshua TAYLOR in August 1774 became bound to Elizabeth SORREL for her faithful execution of the will of her husband Thos. SORRELL and adm. of his estate to MINOR and TAYLOR. Court ordered security. Henry McCABBE and Joseph MOXLEY in November 1778 became that security. McCABBE and MOXLEY obtained a court order for relief and John SPENCER, Ayres SORRELL & Wm. TAYLOR Mercht. in February 1780 became bound to McCABBE & MOXLEY as counter security. TAYLOR becoming uneasy in April 1782 obtained a court order for relief and Wm. LANE with John SPENCER and Ayres SORRELL since deceased became bound for his indemnification. In May now last past ordered that the above bound Robert STEPHENS, Thomas BEATY & Edwin FURR become bound to LANE for his indemnification. Witness: W. ELLZEY, Chas. BINNS.

Bk:Pg: 01:744 Date: 9 September 1769

Tunos STOLE & wife Elizabeth of Loudoun to John HILL Surrender of lease on 200a in Loudoun including the plantation house where STOLE now lives (lease for lives on Guider STOLE, John STOLE and Magdelen STOLE granted Tunos by Kitchen PRIM of Bute Co. NC dated 11 October 1768). Witness: John OBRIEAN, Anthony RUSSELL, Mary STAULL, Benjamin MORE, Ludwick SPLACE [see below]

Bk:Pg: 01:745 Date: 27 February 1770

Assignment. I sign this within mentioned deed all my right and title to Daniel FISHER or his eares. Signed by John HILL. Witness: James PATTERSON, Adam READER.

Bk:Pg: 01:746 – 01:748 Date: 30 May 1822

John SHAW of Leesburg to Peter ISH of Leesburg. Lease for 999y of lot on Market Street in Leesburg adj Back St. [no witness signatures]

Bk:Pg: 01:749 – 01:750 Date: 27 October 1802

John SPENCER & wife Feby to Isaac WYCOFF. Bargain and sale of 97a adj John SPENCER, Thomson BEACH. Witness: Eden B. MOORE, Thos. COCKERILL, Cornelius WYCKOFF. *Proven 9 May 1803 by E. B. MOORE & Cornelious WYCOFF.*

Bk:Pg: 01:751 Date: 21 January 1782
John H. SORRELL of Loudoun to William LANE Junr. of Loudoun. Bill of sale for negroe slaves Jack aged about 45, Harry aged about 23, Celah aged about 26 with her future increase. Also one horse. Witness: Beatis DORSEY, John BOSS. *Proven 12 August 1782 by Bates DORSEY.*

Bk:Pg: 01:752 – 01:753 Date: 1 January 1793
Abraham STATLER of Loudoun to John STATLER of Loudoun. Assignment of lease for unexpired term (George William FAIRFAX, Gent. in leas[e] dated 10 April 1759 granted lease to Stephan HARLING, who assigned lease dated 6 August 1798 to Abraham). Witness: James WHITE, James McKAMIE, [Fillib ŬNGERFERE – name in German] *Proven 8 April 1793 by J. McKIM & P. UNKEFERE.*

Bk:Pg: 01:754 – 01:755 Date: 24 June 1820
Aaron SANDERS of Loudoun to Simon A. BINNS of Loudoun. Release of mortgage of 20 October 1815 for 120a devised by John A. BINNS dec'd to Mary Ann BINNS daughter of late Simon A. BINNS, land devised by his father Charles BINNS dec'd to Simon (Deed Book T, page 117). Mary Ann is now 21y of age and conveyed to Aaron all her rights to 33a in the mortgage. Witness: Lee W. DENHAM, E. G. HAMILTON, Levi C. CORDELL. Proven 8 September 1820 by E. G. HAMILTON, Proven 13 Oct by Lee W. DENHAM.

Bk:Pg: 01:756 – 01:757 Date: 30 March 1788
Robert STEVENS &wife Hannah of Feyatte Co. Pa to David KING, sadler. Bargain and sale of lot on south side of Leesburg on Carolina Road adj Mat WEATHERBY, George HAMMATT. Witness: Jos. STEPHENS, Joseph STEPHENS Jr. James STEPHENS. *Proven 14 October 1788 by Joseph STEPHENS & Jo. STEPHENS Jr.*

Bk:Pg: 01:758 Date: 6 November 1771
John SHEPPEY/SHIPPEY/SHEPPEN & wife Judah of Cameron Parish in Loudoun to John ROBERTS. Assignment of lease of 270a (lease for lives on John SHEPPEN, Samuel SHEPPEN his eldest son & Robert CARTER of Williamsburgh from Robert CARTER dated 16 October 1767). Witness: John TYLER, Edward ATTERBERY, Thomas CLAYTON.

Bk:Pg: 01:759 – 01:760 Date: 7 June 1785
Joseph SMITH of Loudoun to Thomas REEDER of Loudoun. Lease (unexpired term) of 75a on branches of Goosecreek. Witness:

Joseph BURSON, Isaac VOTAW, Samuel NICKOLS. *Proven 8 August 1785 by Isaac VOTAW & Joseph BURGOYNE* [BURSON?].

Bk:Pg: 01:761 – 01:762 Date: 14 May 1814
Winifred SMITH and Charles SMITH of Loudoun to Emala SMITH (daughter of Charles & granddaughter of Winifred). Gift (in consideration of $1 paid by Edward COE also grandfather of Emala) of negroe girl named Ede about 9 or 10 years of age and a negroe child Julia and all their future increase. Witness: S'n. BLINCOE, Philip COE, Robert COE, David J. COE. *Proven 16 May 1814 as to Charles SMITH by S. BLINCOE.*

Bk:Pg: 01:763 – 01:765 [top] Date: 19 March 1778
William SANDERS planter of Loudoun & wife Rachel to Nehemiah DAVIS of Fairfax Co. Bargain and sale of 100a adj Thomas LEE Esqr., ASHTON's paton. Witness: Will. LANE, Alex'r. CATLETT, Wm. HEADON. *Proven 14 September 1778 by Geo. SUMMERS & Hardage LANE.*

Bk:Pg: 01:765 [bottom] Date: __ Jul 1817
Certificate of examination for Ruth SMITH the wife of John SMITH for deed of 7 Jul 1817 to Presley SAUNDERS. [see next entry]

Bk:Pg: 01:766 – 01:767 Date: 1 Jul 1817
John SMITH & wife Ruth of Loudoun to Presley SAUNDERS Jr. of Loudoun. Bargain and sale of lot in Leesburg on S side of Markett St. adj. Chs. DRISH, Jno. LITTLEJOHN, Thos. R. MOTT (½ of lot sold to SAUNDERS & SMITH as tenants in common by Rich'd. H. HENDERSON, Deed Book 2R, page 336). Witness: Pressley FOLEY, R. J. FLINN, Thomas M. WALLER.

Bk:Pg: 01:768 Date: 13 March 1815
Agreement from Frederick STONEBURNER to Wilson Carey SELDEN. Conveys interest in tract near Leesburg on which his father Jacob STONEBURNER died possessed to indemnify him with securities Richard BROWN and John YOCUM in his undertaking as Admr. of his brother Godfrey. Witness: William CHILTON, E. OFFUTT.

Bk:Pg: 01:769 – 01:770 Date: 14 April 1814
Charles SMITH to Ann SMITH & Emala SMITH. Gift ($1 paid by Edward COE their grandfather) of farm animals, furniture, household items. Witness: S'n BLINCOE, Philip COE. *Proven 16 May 1814 by S. BLINCOE.*

Bk:Pg: 01:771 – 01:772A Date: 4 June 1798
Benjamin SMITH of Fayette Co. Pa to James CHANNEL of Middleburg. Bargain and sale of ½a Lot No. 15 in Middleburg at intersection of Madison & Federal St. (to pay yearly rent to Leven POWELL). Witness: Leven POWELL, Jesse McVEIGH, Joseph PATTERSON, John McFARLAND, Andrew SMARR. Deed from Leven POWELL dated 9 August 1798 with witness Jesse McVEIGH. Proven 10 September 1798 by Burr POWELL & Jesse McVEIGH.

Bk:Pg: 01:773 – 01:774 Date: 24 May 1797
Henry SAGLE & wife Darkey of Loudoun to John Alexander BINNS of Loudoun. Bargain and sale of 57¾a adj Anthony SOUDER, John COMFOR, Geo. MAN & Frederick COOPER (Henry bought of Hoe & Little). Witness: Evan GRIFFITH, John LITTLEJOHN, Samuel MURREY, Chs. BENNETT. Certificate of examination for Darkey requested 24 May 1797 to be carried out by Samuel MURREY & John LITTLEJOHN, Gent. *Proven 11 September 1797 by BENNETT.*

Bk:Pg: 01:775 – 01:777 Date: 11 May 1811
Andrew SMARR & wife Lydia of Middleburg to James KINCHELOE of Fauquier Co. Bargain and sale of Lots No. 39 & 40 in Middleburg. Witness: A. GISBON, Thos. A. HEREFORD, Burr POWELL. Certificate of examination for Lydia dated 28 August 1811 returned by Burr POWELL, Leven LUCKETT. *Proven 9 September 1811 by Burr POWELL & 19 September 1837 by Thos. A. HEREFORD.*

Bk:Pg: 01:778 – 01:779 Date: 3 April 1816
Harriot STEPHENS of Loudoun to Joseph REID of Culpeper Co. Va. Bill of sale for household items. Witness: N. C. WILLIAMS, Thomas HERBERT, A. REID. *Proven 8 April 1816 by A. REID.*

Bk:Pg: 01:780 – 01:781 Date: 5 January 1801
John SPENCER & wife Phoebe of Loudoun to John SPENCER Junr. of Loudoun. Bargain and sale of 82a on north fork of Broad Run. Witness: Jos. LEWIS, Step'n. BEARD, [torn] LEWIS. *Proven 12 January 1801 by Jo. LEWIS & Stephen BEARD.*

Bk:Pg: 01:782 – 01:784 Date: 20 March 1811
Andrew SMARR & wife Lydia of Middleburg to Francis W. LUCKETT. Trust for debt to John McIVER using whole of two adjoining ½a lots occupied at present by SMARR in Middleburg (purchased by SMARR of Thomas A. HEREFORD & conveyed by the late Col. Leven POWELL) subject to annual ground rents. Witness: William MURRAY, Burr POWELL. Certificate of

examination for Lydia taken 20 Mar by Burr POWELL, Leven LUCKETT. *Proven 8 April 1811 by B. POWELL.*

Bk:Pg: 01:785 – 01:786 Date: 14 October 1799
John SINCLAIR & wife Rachel of Loudoun to Saml. SINCLAIR of Loudoun. Bargain and sale of 30½a Lot No. 3 in division of estate of Jno. SINCLAIR dec'd. Witness: Isaac STEERE, Joseph STEERE, Isaac STEERE Junr. *Proven 14 April 1800 by Isaac STEER & Jo. STEER.*

Bk:Pg: 01:787 – 01:788 Date: 29 October 1771
John SHIPPEY & wife Judeth of Cameron Parish to Richard SKINNER. Assignment of lease of 270a (lease for lives on John SHIPPEY, Samuel SHIPPEY and Robert CARTER granted John by Robert CARTER of Williamsburg dated 16 October 1767) including the plantation whereon John now lives. Witness: Jno. TYLER, Abraham EGBERT, Thomas CLAYTON.

Bk:Pg: 01:789 Date: 2 April 1803
Reubin SETTLE & wife Susanna to son Daniel SETTLE. Bargain and sale of 50a with dwelling house adj Ariss BUCKNER, lott where John BLAKER lives. Witness: Israel LACEY, Ariss BUCKNER, Thomas ODEN. *Proven 9 May 1803 by Israel LACEY & Ariss BUCKNER.*

Bk:Pg: 01:790 Date: 2 April 1803
Reubin SETTLE & wife Susanna to son Newman SETTLE. Bargain and sale of 50a adj Moses JAMES. Witness: Israel LACEY, Ariss BUCKNER, Thomas ODEN. *Proven 9 May 1803 by Israel LACEY & Ariss BUCKNER.*

Bk:Pg: 01:791 – 01:793 Date: 15 October 1803
Nathan SCHOOLFIELD & wife Hannah of Chester Co. Pa, Thomas SCHOOLFIELD & wife Elizabeth, Rebekah SCHOOLFIELD, John SCHOOLFIELD, and Ann SCHOOLFIELD of Loudoun to William SCHOOLFIELD of Loudoun. Bargain and sale of interest in 132a in Loudoun which Thomas SCHOOLFIELD (now dec'd) purchased of Charles VIRT, adj Pi[torn] BALEY dec'd, Joseph LACEY dec'd, John MOORE and John SCHOOLFIELD's part of s'd tract. Witness: Nath'l. SKINNER, Cornelius SKINNER, Jacob ISH, J. DAWSON, John CRISTMAN. *Proven 14 May 1804 by Cornelius SKINNER & Jacob ISH.*

Bk:Pg: 01:794 – 01:796 Date: 27 May 1811
Presley SAUNDERS Junr. & wife Mary of Loudoun to William WRIGHT, bricklayer of Loudoun. Bargain and sale of lot on east side

of the road from Leesburg to Noland's Ferry, being the residue of that lot conveyed to Presley by George NIXON & wife Ann dated 10 September 1810 after deducting the piece sold by Presley to Jno. DODD Jr. dated 16 March 1811. Witness: Saml. M. EDWARDS, Samuel MURREY, Jno. ROSE. Certificate of examination for Mary dated 27 May 1811 returned by Samuel MURREY, Jno. ROSE. *Proven 10 June 1811 by Samuel M. EDWARDS & 12 May 1812 by John ROSE.*

Bk:Pg: 01:797 Date: 20 November 1799

Charles SMITH of Loudoun to Winniford SMITH. Bill of sale for negroes Silvy, Harry, Rachel, Ellick, Sarah and Matilda. Witness: Wm. COLEMAN, Thos. COLEMAN. *Proven 13 May 1800 by William COLEMAN.*

Bk:Pg: 01:798 – 01:804 Date: 2 September 1824

John RUSSELL, aged 68 years and 8 months, appeared in court and made oath that he enlisted for the term of two years on ___ 1781 in Va in a company of horses commanded by Capt. Thomas HUGHES In the Regiment commanded by Col. Anthony WHITE in the line of Va on the Continental Establishment, that he continued to serve in the same corps until the close of the Revolutionary War, when he was discharged from the said service by Col. A. WHITE near to the city of Charleston in South Carolina, that he was at the seige of York & Gloucester, at the surrender of Lord CORNWALLIS in 1781, and was severally wounded with a beyonet in the right leg, that he was subsequently in the Battle fought by Genl. WAYNE against a body of Indians on the 24th of June 1782 in the neighborhood of Savannah in Georgia. That he feels no inconveniences from the wound he received at York Town that he received an honorable discharged, but having unfortunately lost it, he was ignorant that the laws of his country had provided a way by which he might in such case set forth his claim & that he has no other evidences now in his person of his said services excepting the affadivit of Paul SHRY and John HARRIS, hereunto annexed and the affidavit of sundry persons, neighbors of s'd Paul SHRY, testyfying to his fair character, which papers also hereunto annexed. RUSSEL further declares that at the time he was discharged he did not secure any pay for his services or has he rec'd any since, that his employment has been that of a farmer in Loudoun where he has continued to reside since the peace of 1783. Written by Robt. WHITE, Judge of the 10th Judicial Circuit of the Superior Court of Law state of Va. Affadivit of John RUSSELL – I was a resident citizen of U.S. on 28 March 1818 and I have not since that time, by gift, sale or in any manner disposed of my property or any part thereof in the intent to diminish it. I have not nor has any portion in trust for me, any property or securities, contracts, or debts due to me, nor have I any income other than what is contained in the schedule hereto annexed. Real property – none. Personal property – 2 hoes, 2 mattocks, 1 set of shoemaker tools. Debts – none. Occupation – a farmer. His ability to pursue it is very feeble from the increasing infirmities of age, and the injury received by falling into a well while on duty in Georgia, in the service of the U. S. His family consists of himself and wife, who is 54 years of age and in infirm health. They are residing with their five children, Emily aged 37, Jane aged 35, Sally aged 33 (who is married & has three children), Thaddeus aged 28 and Anthony aged 18. These children and their mother live upon a small farm in Loudoun left in trust for the benefit of the mother & children exclusively, and after the death of the mother, the land to vest in the children. The property is in the hands of the trustee and the declarant has no interest in it. Robt. WHITE, Judge of the 10th Judicial Circuit of Superior Ct. values the above property at no more than $3.50. Dated 28 September 1824. Affadivit of Paul SHRY dated 8 June 1824 presented to R. BRADEN states that he entered into the service of the U. S. in 1781 and at the time he joined Col. WHITE's Reg't. of Horse in Petersburg Va, he then and there met with a certain John RUSSEL who was at the time in the service of his county and belonged to said WHITE's Reg't. and he was informed that RUSSEL had assisted in the capture of Genl. CORNWALLIS. They then proceeded from Petersburg with Genl. WAYNE to South Carolina and continued in the service with him about 18 months and were both discharged at the same time without receiving any pay and he further states that the bearer of this certificate is the same John RUSSEL who served in the army with him and rec'd his discharge at the same time that SHRY did. Statement by Richard TAVENNER, Abdon DILLON, Wm. HOUGH, William DODD, Wm. PAXSON, James BEAVERS, Harmon BITZER, John BITZER, William BITZER that they consider Paul SHRY a man of truth. 5 Oct statement signed by A. GIBSON that John HARRISS of Hardy Co. VA made oath that John RUSSEL of Loudoun was a regular soldier in the Troop of Horse in the Army of U. S. under the command of Col. Anthony WHITE and served in the same regiment that HARRISS served. A schedule given in by John RUSSELL an old soldier in the Revolutionary War as follows: two hoes, set of shoemakers tools the whole valued at $3.50 – dated 1 September 1824 and signed by Wm. B. HARRISON.

Bk:Pg: 01:805 – 01:806 Date: 24 December 1766

William REMEY & Demsy CARROLL of Loudoun to John MACCOWN of Loudoun. Assignment of lease of 150a plantation (Willoughby NEWTON on 20 September 1747 granted lease for lives to REMEY (on lives of REMEY, A. MOHUNDRA his mother and Daniel CARROLL son of Demsy CARROLL), 150a plantation in Truro Parish Fairfax County. on 17 October 1752 life of William

Porter CARROL son of Demsy CARROL was added. Assignment of lease on 13 December 1763 made over the same to Demsy CARROLL Junr.) Witness: G. SUMMERS, William Carr LANE, William Barr SEARS. 9 June 1767 proven by Wm. [creased]. 22 April 1768 proven by s'd witnessses.

Bk:Pg: 01:806 [bottom] Date: 21 December 1772

Daniel LUSH from William SMITH. Friend ROGERS – The bearer waits on thee for Wm. SMITH's lot which he bought of me. He have bought it again and want a proper deed made, therefore I have recommended him to thee to do it for him from thy friend &c. Wm. BAKER.

Bk:Pg: 01:807 Date: 12 December 1823

We the legal heirs and representatives of Stephen C. ROSZEL dec'd assign to Anna ROSZEL widow of Stephen C. all our interest in negro slaves (being a part of the slaves of said Stephen C.) – Cyrus, Nancy, Suckey, Betsey, Milley, Peggy, Mahala, Mary, William, Moses, Anderson, Henry & Kitty under condition that Anna shall by deed of manumission legally recorded in Loudoun immediately set free and discharge from her service and services of all the four first names Negroes Cyrus, Nancy, Suckey and Betsey and that she shall by deed of manumission legally recorded secure the freedom of the above named Milly, Peggy, Mahala, Mary, William, Moses, Anderson, Henry and Kitty. The males on or before they shall arrive at age of 25, and the females and their issue on or before they shall arrive at the age of 21. Signed Sarah ROSZEL, Stephen G. ROSZEL, Sarah DONOHOE, Phebe ROSZEL, Stephen W. ROSZEL, Nancy ROSZEL. Witness: Wm. H. DORSEY, Mahlon CRAVEN, Charles B. YOUNG.

Bk:Pg: 01:808 – 01:809 Date: 5 September 1845

John RATRIE & wife Elizabeth B. of Arcoli [Arcola] to George R. PARBURT of Canadaigue, Ontario County, New York. Bargain and sale of 228a being the farm on which RATRIE now resides and being the same in deed dated 21 December 1838 executed by Lewis BERKELEY & wife Frances to RATRIE; being on both sides of the Little River Turnpike Road adj ___ WICOFT, ___ RUSSELL, James LEWIS. Witness: Martha A. RATRIE. Certificate of examination for Elizabeth dated 27 December 1845 returned by Alexr. D. LEE, Beverly HUTCHISON.

Bk:Pg: 01:810 – 01:811 Date: 13 April 1831

Rebecca SHAW of Leesburg to Samuel M. BOSS of Leesburg. Power of attorney to transact business and collect monies, including under the will of her dead husband John SHAW. Net of monies collected by him to retain annually for four years to come, the ¼ part of a note or bond which he now holds of mine & Mary B. SHAW & John SHAW. Witness: William H. JACOBS, C. C. SUTHERLAND, Sidney SHAW. *Proven 11 Jul 1842 by William JACOBS.*

Bk:Pg: 01:812 – 01:813 Date: 12 May 1831

Adam SANBOWER, Christian SANBOWER, Michael SANBOWER and Catharine SANBOWER to Adam KANE surviving executor of Magdalena SHAVER dec'd. Bond on KANE as Exor. has paid and distributed to the first parties who are entitled under the will of SHAVER the sum of $415.38 each. Whereas there will supposedly be for future distribution a sum of between $500 and $1,000, to 1/24th part of which each of the above will be entitled. The above will refund their due proportion of any debts which appear against the estate. Witness: C. W. D. BINNS, Thomas ROGERS, Jas. W. SMITH, Thos. J. MARLOW.

Bk:Pg: 01:814 Date: 11 December 1848

Evritt SAUNDERS to John BAYLEY Sheriff of Loudoun. Evritt now confined to custody of Sheriff on execution in the name of R. S. DOUGLASS & endorsed for the use of Wm. L. POWELL. Bargain and sale (by act of insolvent debtor) of all interest in 360a or 380a adj Mrs. Nelly NEWTON, ___ LEE, ___ AULT, ___ JOHNSON, Leesburg & Georgetown Turnpike road about 2 miles east of Leesburg. [no signature or witnesses]

Bk:Pg: 01:815 – 01:817 Date: 21 November 1849

Jacob STOUTSENBERGER of Loudoun to Thomas SAUNDERS Sheriff of Loudoun. Jacob this day discharged from confinement under relief of insolvent debtors on executions – two at the suit of Romulus R. GRIFFITH, Thomas B. FITZGERALD and Hezekiah C. MAGRUDER Merchants & Partners trading under the name & firm of Griffith, Fitzgerald & Magruder, one at the suit of John H. DUVALL, George NOTHOWER & Michael W. ROGERS Merchants & Partners trading under the name & firm of John H. Duvall & Co., one against Jacob as surviving partner of Jacob STOUTSENBERGER & Samuel STOUTSENBERGER late Merchants & Partners trading under the name & firm of J. & S. Stoutsenberger, one at suit of the firm of John H. Duvall & Co., one at suit of Edward L. NORRIS, one at suit of Thomas HOPKINS, Wm. HOPKINS & Gerard HOPKINS late Merchants & partners trading under the firm of T. W. & G. Hopkins, one at suit of firm of T. W. & G. Hopkins, one at suit of Thomas E. HAMBLETON, Jesse S. HAMBLETON & John A. HAMBLETON late Merchants & Partners trading under firm of Hambleton & Sons, one at suit of Thomas E. HAMBLETON surviving partner of Thomas E. HAMBLETON & Daniel BUCKEY late Merchants & Partners trading under the firm of

Hambleton Buckey & Co., one at suit of Clinton LEVERING & Charles H. CLARKE Merchants & Partners trading under the name and firm of C. Levering & Clarke, one at the suit of Henry D. HARVEY, Thomas J. CARSON, Samuel C. EDES and James ROSS late Merchants & Partners trading under the firm of Harvey, Carson & Co., one at the suit of J. HOPKINS, Samuel HOPKINS, Henry D. HARVEY and James ROSS late Merchants & Partners trading under the firm of J. Hopkins, Brothers & Co. (last three issued in Loudoun 19 November 1849). Bargain and sale under act of insolvent debtor of property conveyed by him in deeds of trust: to Richard H. EDWARDS trustee to secure Philip VINCEL & others dated 24 March 1848, to James W. RUST trustee for benefit of Philip VINCEL & others dated 6 February 1849, to James W. RUST trustee for benefit of Wm. HICKMAN dated 7 February 1849, to A. S. TEBBS trustee for benefit of James A. & George E. SANGSTER Co. & others dated 27 February 1849. [no witness signatures]

Bk:Pg: 01:818 – 01:820 Date: 21 November 1834

Elwood B. JAMES of Loudoun and Thomas T. NICHOLS of Belmount Co. Ohio of 1st part to James P. BRADFIELD of 2nd part and George SAGERS of 3rd part. Release of trust by BRADFIELD on 15 April 1828 for debt to SAGERS using 6a. Witness: John C. NICHOLS, Jesse HOGE, Joshua HOGE. *Acknowledged 8 June 1835 by George SAGER & 10 June 1835 by E. B. JAMES.*

Bk:Pg: 01:821 – 01:822 Date: September 1803

Court order dated Sept Ct. 1803 – On motion of William HOLMES ordered that Jno. SCHOOLEY, Alexander SUTHERLAND, Benjamin H. CANBY, James HAMILTON, Samuel MURRAY and Mathew WEATHERBY view the most convenient way for turning the road from POTTS's Mill on Goose Creek to Leesburg and make report to the court. Report: that the road may be taken out from the top of the hill near where a house formerly stood, and continued along the line between Wm. HOLMES and Alex'r. McMAKIN, the same course and on the same ground that the Court has directed the Carolina Road to be taken along, to the WS corner said HOLMES cleared land where there is a heap of stone, then in a straight course across a piece of said HOLMES' wood land until it intersects the present road at three black oak saplins standing on the side of said HOLMES' fields, without increasing the distance more than 60 yards or very materially injuring the quality thereof provided said HOLMES along the east side thereof through the low ground where the Carolina Road is to go and also cuts or digs a road in the hill near McMAKIN's which he agrees to and promises to do.

Bk:Pg: 01:822 [bottom] Date: ___ 1762
Receipt – 1762 Mr. Thomas PHILLIPS miller – to your assumpsit to pay me forty shillings one rent due from your son John PHILLIPS for the year 1761. Signed E. E. p. Benj. SEBASTIAN.

Bk:Pg: 01:823 – 01:824 Date: ___ 1805
George SHAFFER of Loudoun to Jacob WINE of Loudoun. Assignment of lease of 100a (George William FAIRFAX Esqr. on 1 May 1762 granted SHAFFER lease). Witness: James HAMILTON, Peggy MORGAN, Peggy MATHEWS. *Proven 9 September 1805 by Peggy MORGAN.*

Bk:Pg: 01:825 – 01:829 Date: 20 March 1797
John SHORT and wife Susanna(h) to William PAXON. Bargain and sale of 76a in Catoctan adj Jacob HICKMAN, Reubin HICKSON now Frederick COWPER, George MANN, lot where Joseph BURGOYNE did live (conveyed by TANKERVILLE and Henry A. BENNETT to SHORT, Deed Book W, page 180). Witness: I. BALL, Nathan BALL, Farling BALL Junr. 8 October 1798 proven by Isaac BALL. SHORT acknowledged receipt in full 20 March 1798. Witness: I. Ball, Nathan BALL, Farling BALL Junr. *Proven 8 October 1798 by Isaac BALL.*

Bk:Pg: 01:830 – 01:831 Date: 1 April 1815
Presley CORDELL, Aaron SANDERS & Thos. PHILLIPS Overseers of the Poor to John McCORMICK of Loudoun. Bind Leroi a free mulatto boy a bastard of the age of 13 years as an apprentice. Witness: Evritt SAUNDERS, Nathan MUSGROVE Junr.

Bk:Pg: 01:832 – 01:833 Date: 12 June 1802
Agatha SUNAFRANK of Loudoun to Michael MILLER of Loudoun. Assignment of lease for unexpired term on 86a (lease dated 20 March 1789 from George Wm. FAIRFAX Esqr. to Jacob SUNAFRANK). Witness: Joseph SMITH, Jacob LONG, Frederick SMITH. *Proven 13 September 1802 by Jos. SMITH & Frederick SMITH.*

Bk:Pg: 01:834 – 01:836 Date: 12 April 1825
William SILKETT/SILCOTT of 1st part, Edward VILOETT/VIOLETT of 2nd part and Daniel WITHERS of 3rd part. Trust for debt to VIOLETT using household items. Witness: Snowden BELL, James BYRNE. *Proven 22 October 1825 by Snowden BELL.*

Bk:Pg: 01:837 – 01:842 Date: 19 June 1812
At Superior Court of Chancery in Richmond.
Colin AULD assignee of William WILSON agst James CAVAN as Admr. and James CAVAN and John CAVAN as heirs and

devisees of Patrick CAVAN dec'd, Hugh STEWART, Marion CAMPBELL and William WILSON – in chancery – decree of 26 Feb last is set aside and cause further heard. Ordered that unless the Defendants James and John CAVAN do before 1 Jan next pay the Plaintiff £1802.4.4 with 5% interest from 11 September 1811 with costs that John LITTLEJOHN, John RAMSEY, Thomas SWANN, Robert J. TAYLOR, Richard H. HENDERSON and Barnett HOUGH Commissioner for that purpose appointed to sell lott and house in Leesburg.

Case of John AULD assignee of William WILSON agst James CAVAN as Admr. & James CAVAN & John CAVAN as heirs and devisees of Patrick CAVAN dec'd., Hugh STEWART, Marion CAMPBELL and William WILSON – in chancery – commissioners listed above on 19 June 1812 advertised the sale and on 9 March 1813 at Peers Tavern in Leesburg offered Lot No. 6 with the houses thereon for sale which were bought by Colin AULD. After expenses leaves $1703.75 which has been paid to the Bank of Virginia.

Final decree. Colin AULD assignee of William WILSON agst James CAVAN Admr. and James CAVAN and John CAVAN heirs of Patrick CAVAN dec'd, Hugh STEWART, Marion CAMPBELL and William WILSON; also Marion CAMPBELL against James CAVANS Admr. and heir at law of Patrick CAVAN dec'd., Sarah CAVAN widow of Patrick dec'd, Archibald McLEAN Admr. of James KIRK dec'd, Harriot KIRK heir of James KIRK dec'd, James KIRK an infant son and heir of Robert KIRK dec'd, who with Harriet KIRK was coheir of said James dec'd, Hugh STEWART and Charles J. LOVE; also Mutual Assurance Society agst Fire on Buildings of State of Virginia agst Colin AULD, James DUNLOP and James WILSON, Hugh STEWART as agent and attorney of Marion CAMPBELL, James and John CAVAN heirs and devisees and James CAVAN Admr. of Patrick CAVAN dec'd – 19 June 1812 sale of mortgaged premises. Court are of opinion that the mortgage made by Patrick CAVAN to William WILSON on 5 September 1788 not having been recorded must be postponed to 25 April 1799, from said CAVAN to Hugh STEWART attorney in fact for Marion CAMPBELL since it does not appear that STEWART or his principal had notice, and both mortgages must be postponed to the claim of the Mutual Assurance Society. Ordered that the Marshal of this Court check on the Bank of Virginia for the $1,702.75 deposited therein, that he pay in the first place to the Mutual Assurance Society $247.42 with interest from 31 December 1813 with costs paid by Society, and that the balance be paid to Colin AULD attorney in fact to Marion CAMPBELL.

Bk:Pg: 01:843 – 01:844 Date: 20 February 1818

Thomas SWANN, Robert J. TAYLOR, John RAMSAY, Richard H. HENDERSON, John LITTLEJOHN and Bernard HOUGH, Commissioners acting under the foregoing decree to Colin AULD of Alexandria. Bargain and sale of mortgaged premises in Leesburg known in plan of town by [cut off and smeared]. Witness: Chs. G. ESKRIDGE, Thomas A. MOORE, J. DREAN.

Bk:Pg: 01:845 – 01:846 Date: ___

Administration of estate of Timothy WHELAN of Leesburgh by Maurice DELANY Admx.. Notes: Thos. DAVIS {STUMP's cropper), Philip BYRNES, Robbin HARROL, Joseph LILLY, Jacob LONG, Danl. MILLER, Henry SHORT Jr., Ben PRIN, Philip HAITER, John BYRNEHOUSE, Jeremiagh BYRNES, John DEMMORY, Henry KUENTS, Thomas BEATMAN, Peter BELTS, Isaac EVANS, John LONG, Phillip NEAR, Thomas THOMPSON, Oliver McCLUER, Samuel McFARNE, Henry ADAMS, Cornelius SHAHER [SHAWEN], Jacob AXLINE, Isaac MILLER, Peter WIDDEN, Samuel LILL, John FILLER, Jessey JAMES, John BEATTEY, totaling £90.0.1

Bk:Pg: 01:846 [bottom] Date: 10 April 1801

Benjamin THOMAS of Loudoun to Lewis SUDDATH of Fairfax. Assignment of lease of interest in lease for three lives on 124a leased by Ludwell LEE. Witness: Johnston CLEVELAND, Rhodhom SIMPSON, John MITCHELL.

Bk:Pg: 01:847 – 01:849 Date: 31 January 1801

Owen THOMAS of Fauquier to James L. MITCHELL of Loudoun. Assignment of lease on lease for lives given THOMAS (William HUTCHISON and Nathan HUTCHISON (children of Joseph HUTCHISON and his wife Elizabeth) by Matthew LEE by his attorney in fact Jeremiah COCKERILL dated 27 February 1796 on 158a in Cameron Parish on Horsepen Branch, Bull Run (Deed Book W, page 352). Witness: Wm. ELGIN, Richard NEALE, Wm. T. NEALE, James LAWLER.

Bk:Pg: 01:850 – 01:852 Date: 9 February 1790

William BROWN and George TAVENER of Loudoun Exors. of William HOLMES late of Loudoun to Horatio CLAGGETT Merchant of London, Great Britain. Power of attorney for inheritance of HOLMES from Edward FELL late of Baltimore Md who was the uncle of HOLMES. Witness: Joseph JANNEY, Wm. CRAIG. Oath of Wm. CRAIG & affirm. of Joseph JANNEY (a Quaker) and Sarah HOLMES widow of Edw'd. HOLMES returned 16 February 1790.

Bk:Pg: 01:853 – 01:854 Date: 10 August 1844
Burr WEEKS of Loudoun to Henry H. HAMILTON of Loudoun. Trust for debt to Thomas G. ELLIS of Kentucky using crops, farm items. [no witness signatures]

Bk:Pg: 01:855 – 01:856 Date: 30 September 1831
William WIRE & wife Catharine of Loudoun to James HOEY and William HOEY of Loudoun. Bargain and sale of one rood 20 pole lot (conveyed by David LOVETT 28 February 1821 to WIRE) adj James and William HOEY. Witness: Jacob STREAM, Jacob RENN, Thos. WILKINSON.

Bk:Pg: 01:857 Date: 13 March 1810
To Mr. Charles BINNS Clerk of the court. Please deliver to Mr. Hiram SEATON the deed of trust which Mr. John VIOLETT gave me which I suspect is lying in your office and this my order shall be your sufficient indemnification for so doing. Signed Samuel SINGLETON. Witness: Joshua SINGLETON.

Bk:Pg: 01:858 – 01:859 Date: 28? April 1817
Sampson VIOLET now of Loudoun to Sanford RAMEY Senr. of Loudoun. Bargain and sale of 4a designated as Lot No. 1 in plat of the division of estate of John VIOLET dec'd by commissioners in friendly chancery suit. Witness: S. BLINCOE, Chas. ESKRIDGE, Geo. MAUND. *Proven 14 January 1818 by Chas. ESKRIDGE.*

Bk:Pg: 01:860 – 01:861 Date: 11 November 1791
William VEALE of Loudoun to Nicholas GRYMES Junior of Loudoun. Lease of 100a (part of tract which Thomas BLINCOE leased from Francis KING & Thomas KING of Somerset Co. Md). Witness: Bazil B. ROADS, Thos. McINTOSH, Nicholas GRIMS Senr., John COLEMAN. *Proven 9 April 1792 by Nicholas GRIMES & Thomas McINTOSH.*

Bk:Pg: 01:862 – 01:863 Date: 13 April 1835
Fenton VANDEVANTER now or late of Loudoun to Mason CHAMBLIN of Loudoun. Power of attorney. Witness: John CHAMBLIN, Geo. D. SMITH, Geo. SINCLAIR.

Bk:Pg: 01:864 – 01:867 Date: 28 October 1774
William TATE & wife Ann of New Castle Co. on the River Delaware to William NEILSON of Loudoun. Bargain and sale of 280a (residue of purchase by TATE of John & Rebekah DIXON 1 September 1762, TATE has already sold to William McKNIGHT 29 October 1763). Articles of agreement dated 23 May 1762 between William

McKNIGHT of New Castle Co. Delaware, yeoman and William TATE.

Bk:Pg: 01:868 – 01:871 Date: 24 January 1831

Thomas TRIBBY & wife Deborah of Jefferson Co. Va to Anna GOODIN of Loudoun. Bargain and sale of 12a adj James LOVE and in 1/10th interest in dowerrige of Agnes POULSEN dec'd. Witness: George WILT, Absalom BEANS, John GOODIN. Certificate of examination dated 26 January 1831 for Deborah by David HUMPHREY & Richard WILLIAMS in Jefferson County.

Bk:Pg: 01:872 Date: 22 January 1839

William TAYLOR of Morgan Co. Ohio to John TIMMS of Loudoun. Power of attorney for sale of personal property in Loudoun.

Bk:Pg: 01:873 – 01:875 Date: 6 May 1848

Samuel TORRISON & wife Lydia of Fauquier to Nancey LATHAN/LATHAM of Loudoun. Bargain and sale of two lots in Union with brick house on one and containing ¾a adj Nancy LOVETT, Henry PLASTER; and a western lot adj Samuel DUNKIN, TOREYSON. [no witness signatures] Acknowledged 6 May 1848 before H. SMITH and Asa ROGERS by Samuel & Lydia.

Bk:Pg: 01:876 – 01:878 Date: 17 March 1787

Lewis Ellzey TURNER & wife Theodosia of Loudoun to John KIMBLER Senr. of Loudoun. Bargain and sale of 36a on Elklicking branch adj John GRYMES Esqr. (conveyed to Fielding TURNER Gent by John DISKIN 24 February 1752 recorded in Fairfax Co. and by deed of gift from Fielding to Lewis 30 November 1780 recorded in Loudoun). Witness: John KIMBLER Jr., Moses JAMES, Jacob JAMES, Benjamin HUTCHISON, Jr., William B'd. SEARS, Wm. GUNNELL 3rd, Jer. HUTCHISON.

Bk:Pg: 01:879 [top] Date: ___

Deed of mortgage from A. McVICKER to Thos. L. LEE the 12 day of Nov. 1810 del'd to Ths. SWANN by F. S. GRAY.

Bk:Pg: 01:879 [bottom] – 01:880 Date: 31 October 1846

Mary R. TYLER widow of Edmund TYLER late of Loudoun to John M. ORR [name written over top of William B. TYLER which was marked through yet name appears in rest of document] of Loudoun. Trust using interest in land of Edmund. (Mary R. TYLER on 29 August 1846 executed to Seth SMITH as commissioner in decree of Circuit Superior Court of Chancery made 28 April 1846 in suit of RUSSELL & MINOR and others vs. William GULICK Admr. of

Edmund TYLER and others sold to William B. TYLER Mary's interest in Edmund's land).

Bk:Pg: 01:881 – 01:883 Date: 12 December 1777
Sampson TRAMMEL Junr. of Loudoun to Charles WHITE of Loudoun. Lease of 107½a known as Clerks Folly. Witness: Peter FOREMAN, John ROSE. Proved 11 May 1778 by Peter FOREMAN. Proven 10 August 1778 by John ROSE.

Bk:Pg: 01:884 Date: 27 February 1808
Charles THRIFT of Bourbon Co. Ky to Eli OFFARD [OFFUTT] of Loudoun. Power of attorney in suit of slander against John McCORMICK of Loudoun

Bk:Pg: 01:885 [top] Date: 14 November 1810
On motion of Benjamin H. CANBY, ordered that the Admr. debonis non of William R. TAYLOR dec'd unadministered by Simon TRIPLETT dec'd be committed to the sheriff and what property is found make sale of the same. Signed C. BINNS, Clk.

Bk:Pg: 01:885 [bottom] – 01:886 Date: 28 October 1765
Robert THOMAS and Thomas CONNELL of Loudoun to Henry MOORE of Loudoun. Lease of 150a in Cameron Parish (original lease 8 December 1750 in Fairfax). Witness: Geo. SUMMERS, Fran. SUMMERS.

Bk:Pg: 01:887 Date: 15 December 18__
Sarah TAYLOR widow of Mandly TAYLOR dec'd of Loudoun to George RUST of Loudoun. Bargain and sale of 70a on Blue Ridge. Witness: Saml. BOGGESS, Leven POWELL, Thos. A. HEREFORD. *Proven 10 January 1803 by Samuel BOGGESS, Thomas HEREFORD.*

Bk:Pg: 01:888 – 01:889 Date: 29 March 1825
Anna TYLER, Penelope TYLER, Margaret TYLER, Catharine TYLER, Harriett TYLER, Elizabeth TYLER and Edmund TYLER of Loudoun heirs of John TYLER dec'd late of Loudoun to Charles TYLER of Fairfax County. Power of attorney to sell 500a in Kentucky on branch of Rough Creek adj John HANDLEY's survey of 1,000a. Witness: Amasa RETICOR, Charles RITTICOR, Joseph PYLES. Witnesses proven before Charles G. ESKRIDGE Deputy Clerk 29 March 1825.

Bk:Pg: 01:890 – 01:892 Date: 15 August 1827
James THOMAS of Loudoun to Joseph T. NEWTON. Bargain and sale of 118a (from lands of the late Ricketts & Newton by commissioner circuit court of Alexandria Co.) Humphrey PEAKE & George WIRE to THOMAS). Witness: James GILMORE, James F. NEWTON, Rich. P. LOVE.

Bk:Pg: 01:893 – 01:894 Date: 30 Jul 1811
Peter TOWARMAN/TOWPERMAN & wife Elizabeth of Loudoun to William H. HANBEY of Loudoun. Bargain and sale of 2a on Goose Creek adj HANBEY. Witness: Rich'd. COCHRAN, John KIPHART, Peter MYERS, A. GIBSON. [no signature of wife]

Bk:Pg: 01:895 – 01:897 Date: 11 April 1783
John TURBERVILL, Gent. of Northumberland to John CURTIS planter of Cameron Parish. Lease of 200a. Witness: James LANE, James WHALEY, Benjamin WHALEY. Memo of 11 April 1783 from TURBERVILLE stating he altered the date of the lease so that it may be legally recorded. Witness: James WHALEY, Will. LANE, Benj'n. COCKERILL, Benj'a. TALBOTT.

Bk:Pg: 01:898 – 01:900 Date: 12 February 1776
John TODHUNTER & Margaret TODHUNTER Exors. of John TODHUNTER dec'd to Josias CLAPHAM. Bargain and sale of 411? acres [hold in paper] near Nolands Ferry adj John ELLIOT, David BAILEY. Witness: Wm. GEORGE, John MARTS, Isaac STEERE.

Bk:Pg: 01:901 – 01:902 Date: 16 April 1812
George TAVENER Jr. of Loudoun to William BRONAUGH. Trust for debt to Saml. DUNKIN using 48a (conveyed by Saml. DUNKIN & wife Ann to TAVENNER). Witness: William GALLHER, Samuel BEAVERS, foreign name. *Proven 14 September 1812 by Wm. GALLEHER, Saml. BEAVERS.*

Bk:Pg: 01:903 –01:904 Date: 31 Jul 1815
George TAVENER Jr. to Lewis GRIGSBY and William BRONAUGH of Loudoun. Trust for debt to Joshua PANCOAST using 133a (conveyed to TAVENER by James CARTER & wife Mary 25 April 1815). Witness: James McKINNY, George TAVENNER, Jonah TAVENNER. *Proven 11 March 1816 by Geo. TAVENER.*

Bk:Pg: 01:905 – 01:907 Date: 15 December 1813
Mordicai THROCKMORTON of Loudoun to Thomas A. BROOKE of Montgomery Co. Md. Trust for additional security to BROOKE using 800a on side of Blue ridge. Witness: Thomson F. MASON, R. J. TAYLOR, Joseph SMITH, C. AULD.

Bk:Pg: 01:908 – 01:910 Date: 1 April 1806

Elias THRASHER of Frederick Co. Md to Henry POTTERFIELD of Loudoun. Trust using 45¼a. Witness: Adam COUNTS, John STEERS, Daniel SHOEMAKER. *Proven 14 Oct. 1806 by Adam COUNTS. Proven by Daniel SHUMAKER 8 June 1812.*

Bk:Pg: 01:911 – 01:913 Date: 11 August 1800

Jonas TAYLOR of York Pa & Benjamin H. CANBY of Leesburg Exors. of Thomas TAYLOR to George FAULEY. Bargain and sale of 135a (purchased by Thomas of Mercer BROWN). Witness: Wm. PAXSON, Adam HOUSHOLDER Jr., Lawrence AMOND. *Proven 8 September 1800 by William PAXSON & Adam HOUSEHOLDER.*

Bk:Pg: 01:914 Date: 19 December 1807

Elijah TAYLOR now of Loudoun to Benjamin GRASON High Sheriff of Loudoun. Conveys (for relief of insolvent debtors) rights to 11a which Alexander SUTHERLAND gave his bond to convey to him and he assigned to William TAYLOR on 31 Aug last; also all real property he is entitled to in Wilmington. Witness: S. BLINCOE, S. HAMMAT, John FLOWERS. *Proven 11 Jul 1808.*

Bk:Pg: 01:915 – 01:916 Date: 4 April 1800

Joseph TALBERT/TALBOT of Loudoun of 1st part, John McELHANY of Loudoun of 2nd part & John WILLIAMS of 3rd part. Trust for debt to WILLIAMS using lot in Waterford on W side of main (Water) St. Witness: Burr POWELL, James McILHANY, Richard L. SPARROW. *Proven 10 September 1800 by W. McELHANY & 10 Jul 1801 by Burr POWELL.*

Bk:Pg: 01:917 – 01:918 Date: 10 October 1774

Simon TRIPLETT, merchant of Loudoun to Cumberland WILSON & Alexander CAMPBELL, Merchants of Dumfries, Prince William. Lease for one year of 270a on Goose Creek with double water grist mill (TRIPLETT purchased from Walter WILLIAMS). Witness: Thomas AITKIN, James WEIR, Boyd REED.

Bk:Pg: 01:919 – 01:921 Date: 12 October 1774

Simon TRIPLETT, merchant of Loudoun to Cumberland WILSON & Alexander CAMPBELL, merchants of Dumfries, Prince William. Release on 270a with double water grist mill. Witness: Thomas AITKIN, James WEIR, Boyd REED. [see above deed]

Bk:Pg: 01:922 – 01:924 Date: 12 April 1783
John TURBERVILLE, Gent. of Westmoreland Co. to Benjamin COCKERILL of Cameron Parish. Lease of 130a adj James LANE Senr. Witness: Will. LANE, John [first letters covered] CURTIS. *Proven 14 April 1783 by John CARTER* [CURTIS?] *& John WHEATLY.*

Bk:Pg: 01:925 Date: 6 August 1793
Mr. BINNS, My son neglected to call for the deeds yesterday. Please let him have them both, the deed the Mr. Pierce BAYLY signed by virtue of a power of attorney and that signed by the wives of the BAYLYs as a relinquishment of dower. Thereby you will oblige. Signed David THOMAS.

Bk:Pg: 01:926 – 01:927 Date: 10 February 1776
John TODHUNTER & Margaret TODHUNTER Exors. of TODHUNTER to Josias CLAPHAM. Lease of 411a. Witness: Willi[a]m GEORG[E], John MARTS, Isaac STEERE.

Bk:Pg: 01:928 – 01:929 Date: 17 March 1787
Certificate of Examination for Theodisia TURNER wife of Lewis Ellzey TURNER for indenture of 17 March 1787. Returned 6 April 1787 by Chas. ESKRIDGE, Wm. GUNNELL 3rd.

Bk:Pg: 01:930 – 01:932 Date: 12 October 1796
Thomas TAYLOR & wife Caleb of Loudoun to Henry TAYLOR of Loudoun. Bargain and sale of 1a adj TAYLOR. Witness: Isaac LAROWE, Alex. SUTHERLAND, Jacob SLATZER. [not signed by Caleb] Proven by A. SUTHERLAND & Jacob SLATZER 20 April 1797.

Bk:Pg: 01:933 – 01:934 Date: 29 March 1811
Susannah TALLY (late Susannah GRUBB) Admx. of Isaac TALLY, Ebenezer TALLY & wife Margaret, Robert COCKERILL & wife Prudence, Isaac TALLY & wife Rachel, William TALLY & wife Catherine (children of Isaac TALLY dec'd) to Adam GRUBB. Assignment of lease of 75a. (Isaac dec'd held lease on 75a granted by George William FAIRFAX to Lawrance SWANKS and on lot with revisionary right conveyed by Ferdinando FAIRFAX 26 October 1810 to Susannah). Witness: Ebenezer GRUBB, Bayn SMALLWOOD, Ezekiel SHAMLEN. *Proven 8 April 1811 by E. GRUBB & E. CHAMBLIN.*

Bk:Pg: 01:935 – 01:938 Date: 8 April 1811
Susannah TALLY (alias GRUBB) Admx. of Isaac TALLY dec'd, Ebenezer TALLY, Robert COCKERELL, Isaac TALLY, William

TALLY (heirs of Isaac TALLY dec'd) of Loudoun of the 1st part, Ebenezer GRUBB, Joshua OSBURN Esqr. & Samuel W. YOUNG of Loudoun of the 2nd part, and Adam GRUBB of the 3rd part. Trust for indenture of 29 Mar last as heir Josiah TALLY is still an infant and will release his rights when he reaches his majority. Witness: Bayn SMALLWOOD, Ezekiel SHAMBLIN, Catharine GRUBB, Ebenezer GRUBB Junr. Proven by Ezekiel CHAMBLIN & Ebenezer GRUBB Jr. 12 November 1811 and ordered certified.

Bk:Pg: 01:939 – 01:941 Date: 17 January 1835

John THROCKMORTON of the 1st part, Rush CHAMBLIN of the 2nd part and Thomas BOGUE Commissioner in the case of James CAMBELL vs Ann W. McFARLING of the 3rd part. Trust for debt using 25a. Witness: Wm. BRADFIELD, James ALLDER, Alfred SHIELDS. Memo dated 25 January 1837 by T. ROGERS Commissioner – I acknowledge the payments of the bonds secured by the foregoing deed of trust they having been made to R. H. HENDERSON.

Bk:Pg: 01:942 – 01:943 Date: 26 October 1790

Henry TOAP of Rockingham Co. Va to Michael BOGER of Loudoun. Assignment of lease (lease of 12 September 1765 from George William FAIRFAX Esqr). Witness: [name in foreign language], Adam SNELL, Jeremiah PURDUM.

Bk:Pg: 01:944 Date: 3 January 1802

Josiah WEADON of Loudoun to Richard WEADON of Loudoun. Bill of Sale for negro woman Ell aged about 26y and a mulatto girl named Winny aged about 4y and a mulatto child named Rose about 3m old (the children of Ell). Witness: Wm. BRONAUGH, George LOVE. *Proven 8 February 1802.*

Bk:Pg: 01:945 Date: 29 May 1801

Mary WEST of Loudoun to Samuel HOUGH of Loudoun. Bill of Sale for mulatto woman Hannah (for 7y from 1st day of Ja'y last past) and her two children Barsheba (until 21y old, b. 9 September 1789) and Susannah (until 21y, b. 11 June 1799). Witness: Amos THOMPSON, Elizabeth SHRYOCK, Susanna SRYOCK. *Proven by Amos THOMPSON.*

Bk:Pg: 01:946 – 01:947 Date: 13 August 1799

Robert WYNN of Loudoun to Mary GREGG. Assignment of lease (lease for three lives from Denny FAIRFAX in 1787 except that part granted to Cornelius KATING). Witness: Thomas GHEEN, John ADAMS, John MUDD. Proven 13 January 1800 by Thos. GHEEN & Jno. ADAMS

Bk:Pg: 01:948 Date: 10 June 1811
Report of Commissioners for the sale of the 150a lease land of William WILDMAN (sold to him by Geo. W. FAIRFAX for term of five lives) to William SMITH. Signed Jesse JANNEY, Geo. TAVENER, R. BRADEN.

Bk:Pg: 01:949 – 01:951 Date: 26 September 1811
Richard WILLETT of Loudoun to Robert BRADEN of Loudoun. Assignment of lease of 150a (from Geo. W. FAIRFAX 1 May 1762 to Joseph MYERS who sold to Thomas CRAFT who sold to WILLETT). Witness: Jos. BRADEN, George WILLETT, Henry ACTON. *Proven 14 October 1811 by George WILLETT, Henry ACTON.*

Bk:Pg: 01:952 [top] Date: 18 April 1823
Jacob WALTMAN, Jacob WATERS & Nicholas ROPP settled with Levi PRINCE Exor. of Samuel WALTMAN dec'd his executorial accts. and bond themselves to discharge PRINCE of all claim they may have against him as Exor. Witness: John WHITE, Ebenezer GRUBB, John S. MARLOW.

Bk:Pg: 01:952 [bottom] - 01:953 Date: 20 October 1800
Please to let the bearer Asa MOORE take the deed from WILLIAMS to me out of the office in order to get WILLIAMS to acknowledge it before some other witnesses that will attend Court. Signed Thomas MOORE. Please to deliver the within mentioned deed to Abner WILLIAMS. Signed Asa MOORE, dated 20 October 1800. WILLIAMS to MOORE deed withdrawn – see order within. Proven by Jno. JANNY & del'd Asa MOORE to get reacknowledged 27 March 1801.

Bk:Pg: 01:954 Date: 1 February 1801
George WILKINSON & wife Rachel of Loudoun to Peter STUMP. Trust using one negro man slave named Saml., one negro girl named Patty (which slaves Rachel hath for and during her natural life by an agreement entered into by s'd. George WILKINSON & John T. CARTER of Westmoreland Co.), horses, cattle, hogs, furniture, household items. Witness: William FIELD, Samuel STUMP, Benjamin STUMP.

Bk:Pg: 01:955 – 01:956 Date: 27 January 1814
Alexander GOOD of Loudoun to A. GIBSON. Trust for debts to Andrew MORTON & Nicholas KILE using horse and furniture, crops. Witness: Jas. SIMPSON, John UPP, Thos. WEEKS. *Proven 8 August 1814 by ___.*

Bk:Pg: 01:957 – 01:959 Date: 26 Jan 1816
Daniel GLASSCOCK to William GLASSCOCK & John GLASSCOCK. Bargain and sale of house and 1 acre lot in Hillsborough. Witness: Stephen GLASSCOCK, Charles GLASSCOCK, James GLASSCOCK. Proven by Charles GLASCOCK & James GLASCOCK 12 August 1816 and ordered to be certifyed.

Bk:Pg: 01:960 – 01:961 Date: 23 August 1814
James GRADY of Loudoun to Edward B. GRADY of Loudoun. Bargain and sale of ¾a on turnpike road adj James GRADY, Isaiah ROMINE. Witness: Jno. L. DAGG, Susen GRADY, Ury GRADY, Mary GRADY.

Bk:Pg: 01:962 – 01:963 Date: 11 March 1833
Timothy PADGET & wife Elizabeth of Loudoun to Baily PADGET of Fairfax Co. Bargain and sale of 112a (deed of settlement proven by John DISKINS conveyed to Mary TEBBS in 1748 in Prince William and on 3 February 1763 conveyed by James TEBBS who intermarried with Mary to Francis PADGET on 21 April 1763 then from Francis to Timothy). Witness: Thomas SETTLE, Nelson SETTLE, A. S. LANE. *Proven by Thomas SETTLE & Nelson SETTLE 14 October 1833.*

Bk:Pg: 01:964 – 01:965 Date: 21 November 1834
Jacob NICHOLS of Frederick Va, William YOUNG of Loudoun, and Thomas T. NICHOLS of Bellmont Co. Ohio to James F. BRADFIELD & wife Elizabeth of Loudoun. Bargain and sale of ___a (indenture of 6 April 1829 conveyed [100a per recorded deed] to YOUNG and NICHOLS to secure debt of Jacob NICHOLS, BRADFIELD has paid in full). Witness: John C. NICHOLS, Jesse HOGE, Joshua HOGE. Acknowledged by Jacob NICKOLS in Frederick Co. 9 May 1835.

Bk:Pg: 01:966 – 01:967 Date: 25 December 1837
Abraham SKILLMAN & wife Delia of Loudoun to Benjamin RUST of Loudoun. Bargain and sale of 1 stere of land where SKILLMAN now lives being separated by an alteration made in the road leading from Beaverdam Bridge to Northfork Meetinghouse. Acknowledged and certificate of examination for Delia before John SIMPSON, Friench SIMPSON 24 February 1838.

Bk:Pg: 01:968 – 01:970 Date: 30 March 1826
George GIBSON of Loudoun to Daniel WITHERS of Fauquier Co. Trust for debt to Amos DENHAM using 8½a (conveyed to GIBSON by Elijah VIOLETT & wife Phebe) adj Jos. LEWIS, Hiram SEATON and ___ POWELL whereon Joseph WRIGHT and Gainer PIERCE

now live. Witness: Burr WEEKS, Jas. HARL, David B. DENHAM. Proven 3 August 1826 by Burr WEEKS and David DUNHAM as to Geo. GIBSON.

Bk:Pg: 01:970 [bottom] – 01:971 Date: 8 Jul 1808
John GIST and Thomas GIST of Loudoun to Johnston CLEVELAND. Bill of sale for negro woman Lucy, negro boy Alfred, negro boy Harry, negro boy Charles, negro boy Sanford (boys are children of Lucy). Witness: Ths. N. BINNS, James GILES. *Proven 18 February 1809 by Thos. N. BINNS.*

Bk:Pg: 01:972 – 01:973 Date: 4 April 1806
Heirs and representatives of John FALLY dec'd (Anthony FALLEY, Henry FALLEY, Daniel STONEBURNER, Peter FALLEY) agree to sell John's land. Witness: John HAMILTON, Stephen DANIEL, John ROBERTSON, David ORISON. Agreed to by Jacob SPRING & wife Elizabeth on 6 May 1806 in Muskingum Co. Ohio. Proven 8 September 1806 by Jno. HAMILTON as to Anthony FALLEY, Henry FALLEY & D'l. STONEBURNER. Proven 10 June 1811 by Stephen DANIEL & John ROBERTSON as to Anthony FALLEY, Henry FALLEY & Daniel STONEBURNER.

Bk:Pg: 01:974 – 01:976 Date: 8 Jul 1816
John GREGG & wife Pheby of Loudoun to brother Thomas GREGG of Loudoun. Bargain and sale of 34½a (his share willed by Thomas GREGG now dec'd to Levi GREGG his son & Thomas GREGG & John GREGG). [no witnesses signatures] Acknowledged by John and Phebe 19 October 1816.

Bk:Pg: 01:978 [top] Date: 5 May 1781
Sarah GIST of Loudoun to Hanson LEWIS (alias GIST) of Loudoun. Bill of sale of negro woman Hannah BEANS. Witness: George LEWIS, William GIST. 11 June 1781 proved by Geo. LEWIS & cert'd.

Bk:Pg: 01:978 Date: 15 September 1798
John GIST & Benjamin HUTCHISON of Loudoun to Charles SHEPHERD of Loudoun. Bill of sale of negro girl slave Mint aged ___ years. Sebastian LOESH, Isaac LAROWE, John GILHAM, Francis HUGHES.

Bk:Pg: 01:979 Date: 8 November 1801
James N. FISHBACK & wife Sarah to Josiah CARR & William H. POWELL. Trust using 1/3 part of plantation on which we now live until the proceeds thereof will discharge the debt. Authorises Wm. H. POWELL who as Guardian now possesses the other two thirds of

s'd plantation to take trust of other 1/3. Witness: Jon'a. FOUCH. *Proven 12 January 1802 by Jonathan FOUCH.*

Bk:Pg: 01:980 Date: 7 February 1834

Relinquishments of two negroes belonging to estate of (Henry about 70y old, Bailley between 40-50y old) Amos DENHAM dec'd by heirs Margaret HORTON, Mary DENHAM, Amy DENHAM, Elizabeth DENHAM, Edmonia DENHAM, Amos DENHAM & Charles DENHAM to Mrs. Amy E. DENHAM. Witness: D. B. DENHAM, O. DENHAM.

Bk:Pg: 01:981 – 01:984 Date: 18 December 1830

Henry D. HALE & wife Frances, Francis T. HALE & wife Olevia, Frances P. HALE, George LOVE & wife Mary, Daingerfield FAUNTLEROY & wife Margaret P. all of Fauquier to Richard COCHRAN of Middleburg. Bargain and sale of interest in lot in Middleburg (William HALE by his will in Fauquier devised lot in Middleburg to three sons George, Henry D. and Francis T. in fee simple subject to incumbrance during the life of his wife Elizabeth HALE and whereas George departed life leaving others as the lawful heirs). Acknowledged by Daingerfield FAUNTLEROY 8 May 1837 before A. GIBSON, Hamilton ROGERS. Certificate of examination for Margaret P. FAUNTLEROY 8 May 1837 returned by A. GIBSON and Hamilton ROGERS. Certificate of examination for Olivia D. HALE 26 January 1841 returned by A. GIBSON, Hamilton ROGERS. 4 August 1837 returned. 12 March 1838 handwriting of F. T. HALE proved by B. WEEKS. 10 March 1840 proved writing of F. T. HALE by Lloyd NOLAND. 13 September 1840 proved writing of F. T. HALE & Frances P. HALE by Jno. W. PATTERSON & ordered to be certified.

Bk:Pg: 01:985 – 01:986 Date: 10 May 1796

John POTTS to James McILHANY. Bargain and sale of 182½a between Short Hill and Blue Ridge adj William SMITH, Ezekiel POTTS, William OSBURN. Witness: Rich'd. GRIFFITH, Joseph TRIBBEY, James GRIFFITH, Joseph HOUGH, Joseph WILLIAMS. *Proven 9 [?] May 1796 by R. GRIFFITH & Jos. TREBBE.*

Bk:Pg: 01:987 – 01:988 Date: 2 June 1770

John MARSELLES of Hopewell, Hunterdon Co. New Jersey to Peter HOFF of Prince William Co. Power of attorney to receive from Elnathan MOORE money from bonds. Witness: Daniel CLARK, Neill McGILL.

Bk:Pg: 01:989 – 01:891 Date: 28 April 1817
Sampson VIOLET of Dellaware Co. Ohio but now of Loudoun to Sanford J. RAMEY of Loudoun. Trust for indemnification of 50a in Fourth quarter of Fourth Township and 17th Range of U.S. Military District being N half of Lot No. 22 (Sandford RAMEY Sr. of Loudoun purchased of Sampson all his interest in estate of his father John VIOLETT dec'd and Sampson's wife refuses to relinquish her right of dower). Witness: Z. DULANEY, R. BRADEN, George GRAVES, Joseph CALDWELL.

Bk:Pg: 01:992 – 01:992A Date: 8 February 1820
Christian NISEWONGER of 1st part, Notley C. WILLIAMS of 2nd part and Mary WATERS of 3rd part. Marriage contract - in consideration of impending marriage between Christian and Mary, trust (in event Christian outlives Mary) that all her property be disposed of as she may direct and if she outlives him all his possessions to be used to take care of her. Witness: James CURRELL, Francis CURRELL, John S. CURRELL.

Bk:Pg: 01:993 Date: 10 September 1795
James HEREFORD to Mathew HARRISON Jr. Trust for natural affection he bares towards his niece Juliett HEREFORD to settle and convey a rent in fee simple to be paid by John LITTLEJOHN and for lot adj. Leesburg for life remainder to Juliett. Witness: Charles J. LOVE, George NEWMAN, James NEWMAN. Acknowledged by parties 15 June 1796. Recorded in Deed Book X, folio 103.

Bk:Pg: 01:994 – 01:996 [top] Date: 16 March 1758
Abel JANNEY of Loudoun to Joseph JANNEY of Loudoun. For natural affection and for better maintenance & livelihood of Joseph, gift of 200a on side of short hill being part of patent to Catesby COCKE (2 May 1739) and transferred to Abel JANNY by lease & release on 1 May 1754 (Fairfax Co. Book E, page 205) adj Israel THOMPSON. Witness: E. MASTERSON, Robt. WOOD, Ths. OWSLEY. Acknowledged 14 March 1758 by Abel JANNEY and ordered to be recorded.

Bk:Pg: 01:996 – 01:1000C Date: 4 September 1809
William Sloughton GANTT of Loudoun to Edward S. GANTT of Fairfax. Under Power of Attorney from Edward as Guardian of his children Rachel A. GANTT, Mary S. S. GANTT, Sloughton GANTT and Sarah Ann GANTT to William, did sell in May 1806 to Littleton Dennis TEAKLE of Sommersett Co. Maryland negro slaves the property of the children for their benefit (Rachel's slaves Fender, Tabby, Julia and children; Mary's slaves Martha, Luccy and their

children; Stoughton's slaves Henry, Hannah and their children; and Sarah Ann's slaves George and Rosetta). Under Power of Attorney from Ann Stoughton GANTT of Fairfax to William S. he also sold to TEAKLE land in Sommersett Md for benefit of William S. GANTT himself. William S. is indebted to John H. CANBY, Robert HOUGH, James DAWSON – trust using goods, groceries and hardware in store in Leesburg, slaves Lowther, Nancy, Bennett, Sommersett, Tubman, Josiah, Dilley and her children, Lucey and Leah, Nell and her children, James, George, Harriet and Fanny and Kessey. Includes a schedule of property – slaves, household items returned by Charles Fenton MERCER, Geo. W. BALL, John T. LEE, Wm. CHILTON.

Bk:Pg: 01:1000D – 01:1000F Date: 20 April 1846
Nancy KOONE, Mary Ann KOONE, William McCLAIN & wife Elizabeth (formerly KOONE), Sarah Anne HINES (formerly KOONE) wife of Thomas HINES of Richland Co. Ohio to Nelson CHAMBLIN of Richland Co. Ohio. Power of Attorney for sale of real estate in Loudoun of George KOONE dec'd.

Bk:Pg: 01:1000G – 01:000I Date: 20 November 1848
Peter DEMORY late of Loudoun now deceased by his will bequeathed to Cynthia Ann COE now Cynthia Ann BALL wife of Jarvis BALL of Fayette Co. Indiana $1,000 when she reached 21 years and appointed Edward HARDING Exor. of will. Power of attorney - Cynthia Ann the granddaughter of said Peter DEMORY dec'd appointed Elijah W. COE of Union Co. Indiana as her attorney to receive legacy. Witness: Joseph JUSTICE, Jonathan SHIELD.

Bk:Pg: 01:1000J – 01:1000K Date: 4 April 1796
Zachariah LYON of Loudoun to William CAMPBELL of Frederick Co. Va. Bargain and sale of 215a on ridge between Piney branch and Walnut Cabin branch adj Benjamin JAMES, old mountain road. Witness: Jacob ISH, Israel LACEY, Pierce BAYLY, Wm. P. BAYLY, Noble BEVERIDGE.

Bk:Pg: 01:1000L – 01:1000M Date: 5 April 1796
Zachariah LYON & wife Mary of Loudoun to William CAMPBELL of Frederick Co. Va. Release of 215 acres as above. Witness: Israel LACEY, Pierce BAYLY, Wm. P. BAYLY, Jacob ISH, Noble BEVERIDGE. Proven 11 ___ by P. BAYLEY & [torn] and ordered to be cert'd.

Bk:Pg: 01:1000N – 01:1000P Date: 28 January 1826
Andrew CAMPBELL & wife Jane of Loudoun to Asa ROGERS of Loudoun. Trust for debt to David CARR using one moiety of 140a

where CAMPBELL now lives (other moiety conveyed by trust to Sampson BLINCOE for debt to William CARR). Witness: William CARR, Stephen CAMPBELL, William JOHNSTON.

Bk:Pg: 01:1000Q – 01:1000R Date: 14 September 1802
Mary BAILEY/BALEY wife of Thomas BAILEY of Brook Co. Va and daughter of Adonijah FARNSWORTH of Loudoun to John FARNSWORTH of Loudoun. Bond for her share of estate of father Adonijah sold to John. Witness: John BOND, Rober[t] FARNSWORTH, Samuel FARNSWORTH. 1815 October 14 ret'd. Acknowledged 11 June 1816 by Thomas BAILEY.

Bk:Pg: 01:1000S – 01:1000T Date: 15 May 1823
Samuel HUGHES & wife Elizabeth, Elisha HUGHES & wife Fanny, Matthew HUGHES and Lydia HUGHES of Loudoun to Thomas HUGHES Jr. of Loudoun. Power of Attorney to sell land of their father Thomas HUGHES dec'd. Witness: Stacy TAYLOR, Jesse SILCOTT. 14 November 1823 rec'd.

Bk:Pg: 01:1000U – 01:1000W Date: 2 November 1805
Joseph CARR & wife Delia of Loudoun to Baptist Society composing Goose Creek Church. Bargain and sale of 1a on N side of turnpike road near Logan's shop leading from Ashby's Gap to Alexandria. Witness: Wm. BRONAUGH, Saml. BOGGESS, William FOWKE. *Proven 10 February 1806 by Saml. ROGERS, William FOWKE.* Certificate of examination of Delia dated 8 February 1806 by Wm. BRONAUGH, Ben GRAYSON.

Bk:Pg: 01:1000X – 01:1000Y Date: 2 October 1793
David THOMAS & wife Catherine of Berkley Co. Va to Jenkins PHILLIPS of Jefferson Co. Ky. Writ of dower executed on Thomas PHILLIPS & David JAMES by said David THOMAS & Catherine for land in Loudoun in possession of said PHILLIPS and JAMES upon which a recovery was had with others pending in Prince William. Jenkin PHILLIPS purchased the land from ___ SHREVE and will have right to recover damages against SHREVE. Jenkins is giving up his rights of recovery for £30 and title to the 1/3 part of land. Witness: John HELM, Thos. PHILLIPS Jr., Wm. BOYD, Leven POWELL Jr., James BARTLETT, Moses BOTTS. *Proven 9 December 1793 by Lev. POWELL Jr. Proven 13 January 1794 by James BARTLETT.*

Bk:Pg: 01:1000Z – 01:1002 Date: 18 May 1774
Absolom FOX of Loudoun to John BERRYMAN of Lancaster. Bargain and sale of 500a (FOX bought of BERRYMAN & his wife

Martha by lease/release dated 5 and 6 Feb 17_5 [cut off]). Witness: Stephen DONALDSON, Wm. BAKER.

Bk:Pg: 01:1003 – 01:1004 Date: 7 April 1803

Henry JENKINS of Loudoun to Thomas Ludwell LEE and Landon CARTER Esquires Exor. of George CARTER dec'd. Trust using 250a conveyed from LEE and CARTER. Witness: Jno. MATHIAS, Thomas FOUCH, Samuel DONOHOE. Proven 16 April 1806 by Tho. FOUCH, James MATTHIAS.

Bk:Pg: 01:1005 – 01:1007 Date: 19 May 1810

James CAMPBELL & wife Ruth of Loudoun to Robert RUSSELL of Loudoun. Bargain and sale of 4a (part of land CAMPBELL obtained by land office treasury warrant No. 2244 issued 9 August 1797) adj ___ BROOKES, ___RAMSEY, ___ CLAYTON, Manor of Leeds, W. L. LEE. Witness: Martin OVERFIELD, George Hawkins ALLDER, John BRARDY. Certificate of examination of Ruth dated 15 October 1810 returned by Stacy TAYLOR, N. C. WILLIAMS. *Proved 10 December 1810 by George H. ALLDER & John BRARDY.*

Bk:Pg: 01:1008 Date: 28 November 1794

Thomas CHINN of Loudoun to friend Thomas WREN of Loudoun. Power of attorney for sale of several tracts of land in Ky. Witness: Anthony ETHELL, William WREN.

Bk:Pg: 01:1009 – 01:10010 Date: 11 August 1809

Washington COCKE of Fauquier to John SPENCER of Loudoun. Bargain and sale of 1,010a (part of 2,020a granted Catesby COCKE and formerly leased to Thomas OWSLEY 13 June 1733). Witness: John PALMER, Pahilip [Philip] PALMER. Proven 9 April 1810 by James ___ & ordered to be certified. Proven 2 May 1831 by Philip PALMER.

Bk:Pg: 01:10011 – 01:10012 Date: 22 May 1772

William MORLAN, joiner of Cameron Parish to Joseph BRIGGS, wheelwright of Cameron Parish. Lease of 153a (Henry Ludwell LEE of Stafford and Richard Henry LEE of Westmoreland leased for lives 200a to MORLAN 4 November 1767). Witness: Chs. BINNS, And'w WALES, S. ROGERS,.

Bk:Pg: 01:10013 – 01:10014 Date: 14 November 1807

William MANN & Charles Fenton MERCER Commrs. in suit of Richard CHESTER & William MASTERMAN Exors. of Daniel MILDRED dec'd. to Isaac HARRIS. Bargain and sale (sale held at James DAWSON's tavern in Leesburg 13 November 1807) of 3a adj McINTYRE, James KIRK now Isaac HARRIS, branch of Tuskorora.

Witness: Jno. MATHIAS, Henry CLAGETT, John CAVANS, Libourn? WILLIAMS, Chs. F. MERCER.

Bk:Pg: 01:10015 – 01:10017 Date: 6 September 1828

Marriage contract between James HILL and Elizabeth WOODFORD widow & relict of William WOODFORD dec'd & Notley WILLIAMS. Elizabeth has right of dower in the Round Hill tract of land and another lot on the mountain at Snickers Gap which are under leases, rights to negro Leven and right of dower to negroes Ned, Phill, Alice and her child Presley Francis and farm animals, furniture. She has several debts as Admx. of estate of her late husband William. Trust using all of the above for administration of will. Witness: Geo. H. ALLDER, Roger CHEW, Wm. ADAMS, Samuel PALMER Jr. *Proven 13 April 1829 by Roger CHEW & Samuel PALMER.*

Bk:Pg: 01:10018 – 01:10019 Date: 2 January 1797

Daniel BISHOP & wife Sarah of Loudoun to Benjamin BERKLEY. Bargain and sale during natural life of Sarah 1/3rd part of all land by will of Barbara BERKLEY devised unto Reuben REED dec'd dated 28 January 1785. Witness: Saml. LOVE, Francis ADAMS, Chs. J. LOVE, Jos. NEWMAN, Thos. BLINCOE. *Proven 10 May 1797 by Thomas BLINCOE.*

Bk:Pg: 01:10020 – 01:10021 Date: 30 August 1795

John HAMPTON & wife Mary, Jesse WILLIAMSON & wife Nancy, Josiah WEADON & wife Jane, Joseph MOORE & wife Cloe to Robert SMARR & Sarah SMARR widow & relict of John SMARR. Bargain and sale of interest in 270a where John SMARR resided until his death (will of John SMARR dec'd to his afs'd children). Witness: Joseph HAMPTON, Saml. HAMPTON, John PRITCHARD, Wm. BRONAUGH Jr., Francis HUME Jr., Richard WEADON.

Bk:Pg: 01:10022 Date: ___ 1785

Barbara BERKLEY of Loudoun to son John REID. Gift of 173a adj Wm. REID, Thomas BROWN, ___ WALKER, Rockey Run. Witness: John WEAVER, William READ, Benj'n. BERKLEY.

Bk:Pg: 01:10023 – 01:10025 Date: 6 October 1812

James CARTER & wife Mary of Loudoun to Samuel PEW and Price JACOBS of Loudoun. Trust for debt to John ONEALE using 133a on Beaverdam branch of Goose Creek (purchased by CARTER from ONEALE). Witness: George MARKS, John ONEALE, Daniel THOMPSON, Wm. BRONAUGH, Francis W. LUCKETT. *Proven 14 December 1812 by Francis W. LUCKETT, W. BRONAUGH.*

Bk:Pg: 01:10026 Date: 6 November 1788
James SANDERS & Gunnell SANDERS of Kentucky to Aaron SANDERS. Power of attorney for money and to sell land they own jointly in Berkley Co. and land James purchased from William SMALL. Witness: Presley SANDERS, Moses SANDERS.

Bk:Pg: 01:10027 – 01:10029 Date: 26 November 1793
Thomas MACINTOSH of Loudoun to Jacob BEAVERS of Loudoun. Assignment of lease of 101a (lease for lives of Henry HOWDERSHELL, Philip HOWDERSHELL his first son and Christian HOWDERSHELL his first daughter dated 21 December 1773; HOWDERSHELL in 1778 sold to MACINTOSH). Witness: Thos. MINOR, James JENINGS, Peter WILTS.

Bk:Pg: 01:10030 – 01:10032 Date: 22 August 1791
Robert McCREA and Robert MEASE Merchants & partners to George EMERY of Loudoun. Release of mortgage of 14 October 1788 of lot at Loudoun and King Sts in Leesburg. Witness: William TAYLOR, Jno. RAMSAY, Alexander WILSON. Receipt of 1 August 1791 witnessed by Stephen EMERY, John HOLMS, Oliver PIERCE.

Bk:Pg: 01:10033 – 01:10037 [top] Date: 4 April 1792
Alexander WILSON late of Plumstead Bucks, Co. Pa. Will dated 24 March 1791 from Bucks Co. Pa. (Executors brother James FARIS and George GADDIS. Inventory to be presented before the 4th of May and an account by 4 May 1793.) Bequeaths plantation in Pa to four grandchildren (William WILLSON, James WILLSON, Alexander WILLSON and Elizabeth WILLSON) to be sold and equally divided and paid when boys are 21y and girl is 18y. Gives granddaughter Elizabeth furniture valued and taken out of her share of the sale, also given all pewter. All money and bonds to be equally divided among grandchildren. Plantation to be rented until loan in Philadelphia is paid. Witness: John CLOSSON Sr., Amos SHAW, Adam DEVISON.

Bk:Pg: 01:10037 [bottom] – 01:10038 Date: 9 September 1805
James WHELAN will rec'd 12 May 1805. At court held 9 September 1805 the court hearing the testimony of subscribing witnesses to last will and testament of James WHELAN dec'd refused to admit the same to record, it appearing to them that he was not of a disposing mind. Will of James WHELAN dated 1 August 1804, estate which brother Timothy WHELAN left him gives ½ to his sister Catharine and other half to be equally divided among his sisters Margaret, Judith and Winnifred. In case of their death to their issue and as my brother Timothy WHALEN supposed that Terrence FIGH was indebted to him by account and it was his request that it should be

given to FIGH. James HAMILTON as Exor. and to act in his place as Exor. of Timothy WHELAN dec'd. Witness: Philip HUFF, David MULL, James HAMILTON.

Bk:Pg: 01:10039 Date: 18 March 1826

Renouncement. Widow of John WILDMAN dec'd declares that she will not accept the provision made by the will of her dec'd husband. Requests that John J. MATHIAS, William THRIFT, Isaac HAWLING & Saml. M. EDWARDS set apart and allot her dower. Witness: Lewis BEARD, C. B. HAMILTON.

Bk:Pg: 01:10040 – 01:10042 Date: 16 Jul 1825

Will of David GOODIN, farmer of Loudoun. Wife Ann given the dwelling house and 1/3 of all his land, two horses, two feather beds and furniture. All the farm where he now lives to his two sons John and David and when David is 21y old to be divided equally between them. Before David of age wife Ann to have the whole farm and apply the profits to the benefit of the family. At her death her 1/3 of land and dwelling house, etc. divided between John and David. Six daughters Maria, Sarah, Rachel, Martha, Elizabeth and Kitty given $600 each when they come of age 21y. Wife Ann and friend Jonah SANDS as Exors. Witness: William BUFFINGTON, Stephen KERRICK. 15 March 1828 – on motion of Ex. Ann GOODIN, ordered that Maria GOODIN, John GOODIN, Rachel GOODIN, Martha GOODIN, David GOODIN, Elizabeth GOODIN, Kitty Ann GOODIN and Jonah SANDS who is also named as Exor. be summoned to appear here second day of April Ct. to show cause why this will should not be admitted to record. 12 March 1828 will presented, Js. LOVE app'd curator with $5,000 bond and Noah HATCHER as security. 14 May on hearing will is rejected. On motion of David GOODEN Admr. of Jane GOODEN dec'd, ordered that James LOVE, Stacy TAYLOR & Jonah NICHOLS settle the estate acct. of said GOODEN and report to the court.

Bk:Pg: 01:10043 – 01:10044 Date: 25 February 1822

Nuncupative will of Joseph EDWARDS of Loudoun (being sick and weak of body). To wife Lydia EDWARDS all estate as for maintainance and education of his four children James EDWARDS, Henrietta EDWARDS, Jonathan EDWARDS & John Thomas EDWARDS. If wife thinks proper to marry than to sell everything and divide equally among children and wife. Wife and Capt. Charles LEWIS as Exors. [no witness signatures] 13 May 1822 on hearing witnesses is rejected & adm'ng granted.

Bk:Pg: 01:10044 – 01:10046 Date: 28 December 1825
Will of Adam STONEBURNER (sick and weak). 13 February 1826 presented to the Court and two of the subscribing witnesses being examined the will was rejected. Will - To wife all the furniture and three horse, some farm items and animals and as much wheat as will serve her & children until next harvest and all the meats. If wife should change her name all is to fall back to his three children. Balance of property to be sold. John MANN as Exor. Witness: John W. CURTIS, John MANN, Mahala RIDENBAUGH.

Bk:Pg: 01:10047 – 01:10048 Date: 1 April 1819
Wm. HOWELL 1 April 1819 rejected. Will of Wm. HOWELL of Loudoun dated 29 April 1816. Sell all personal estate to pay debts and divide equally among children Jesse HOWELL, Abner HOWELL, Abel HOWELL, Margaret WEST. To son Abner for his assistance during my infirmity all his real estate consisting of a lease for lives of 116a where he now resides. Son Jesse HOWELL and friend Nathan NICHOLS Sr. as Exors. Witness: Edward CUNARD Jr., Jonathan FARNSWORTH, John BISHOP.

Bk:Pg: 01:10047 and 01:10049 Date: 9 October 1826
Mrs. Eliz'a SMITH's will 9 October 1826 proved by Chs. BINNS one of the subscribing witnesses & ordered to be certified. Will of Elizabeth SMITH of Leesburg dated 24 January 1824. To daughters Margaret and Ellanor the real property being ½ of the house and lot where she now lives. Friend Doctr. Jno. T. WILSON named as Exor. Witness: Saml. M. EDWARDS, C. BINNS.

Bk:Pg: 01:10050 – 01:10052 Date: 9 August 1784
Will of William SUDDARTH of Loudoun dated 5 June 1784 (sick and weak of body). To son Lawrence SUDDARTH one negro woman named Jenny to him and his heirs male lawfully begotten but for want of such to go to the next male heirs, also gives horses, furniture, clothes. To daughter Mary Ann SUDDARTH one negro girl Jenny & her increase but for want of such to go to the next male heir, horses, furniture. To grandson Owen SUDDARTH the first born negro child which shall or may be born of my negro girl Sibby, also gun. To grandson William SUDDARTH one negro girl named Sibby & her increase (except as above), also gun which once belonged to his father. To daughter Ann GILLMORE one negro girl Flora, horses, furniture. To niece Ann PEYTON daughter of John SMITH & wife Margaret £20. Remainder of stock and estate to son Lawrence SUDDARTH, daughters Ann GILLMORE and Mary Ann SUDDARTH equally. To grandsons Owen SUDDARTH and William SUDDARTH (sons of my son William dec'd) a horse when they are of lawful age (provided by son Lawrence & Robert GILLMORE). Friends Hardage LANE and Abraham BUSH as Exors. Witness: Geo. SUMMERS,

Joseph SMITH, Sarah DOYAL. Proven 9 August 1784 by witnesses, $2,000 bond.

Bk:Pg: 01:10053 [top] Date: 9 December 1793

George HEAD personally appeared before me and made oath that during the last days of Joshua THATCHER dec'd wheelwright late of this county he heard Joshua declare that it was his will if he died of this sickness that his son Silvester should have his shop and all his tools with every thing else he was possessed of. Signed John LITTLEJOHN, 9 December 1793.

9 December 1793 – THATCHER widow personally appeared before me and made oath that on the morning of the day her late husband Joshua THATCHER died he called his son Silvester to his bedside and told him to take good care of his shop & tools saying I give you them & every thing else that I have only take care of your mother & sister. Signed John LITTLEJOHN.

Bk:Pg: 01:10053 [bottom] Date: ___

Will of Jesse WADE of Loudoun dated 25 December 1809. To son James WADE negroes Sarah, Henry & Mary. Remainder of property to his wife Mary WADE. Robert FLEMING of Montgomery Co. Md as Exor. Witness: John A. HARRISS, John JEFFERSON, Mark BLINCOE, Henry SUMMERS.

Bk:Pg: 01:10054 Date: ___

Will of John MARTIN of Loudoun dated 9 February 1805 (weak of body). To Christiana CLOUD alias Christiana MATHEWS for service rendered the whole of his personal property after paying debts. Witness: Abner CRAVEN, Thomas WARDER.

Bk:Pg: 01:10054 [bottom] - 10056 Date: ___

Will of John HANBY of Loudoun dated 10 May 1798 (weak of body). To wife Mary HANBY the use of my plantation during her life with two works horses and two cows and all household furniture, sheep, and furniture that was her property at their marriage. To three nephews Elihu HARDING, Job HARDING and William HARDING my plantation after the death of my wife, to be sold and equally divided. To Elihu HARDING my silver watch. To Job HARDING my riding saddle. To William H. HARDING my gold ring which was the property of my grandfather. To my sister Mary HARDING £20. Nephew William H. HARDING as Exor. Witness: Chas. BENNETT, John BINNS. Proven 14 January 1799 by C. BENNETT & cert'd. W. H. HARDING q'd. Exor. bond & sec'y given, $3,000 J. ALEXANDER.

Bk:Pg: 01:10057 – 01:10058 [top] Date: 11 February 1805
Will of John HATCHER of Loudoun dated 10 October 1801. To wife Sarah HATCHER all the estate and income during her life. To son Noah HATCHER the plantation whereon I now live. To children Joshua HATCHER, Ann DILLON, William HATCHER and John HATCHER the remainder of said estate equally. Son Noah HATCHER and friend George TAVENNER Senior as Exors. Witness: Joseph ROBERTS, Stephen KERRICK, Levi HOLLINGSWORTH. Proven 11 February 1805 by Jos. ROBERTS and certified. Noah HATCHER qualified Exor. with $1,000 bond with Jos. ROBERTS and George TAVENNER securities.

Bk:Pg: 01:10058 [bottom] Date: ___
Will of Patrick CRANEY of Culpeper Co. dated 31 May 1798 (very weak of body). To brother William CRANEY's children and brother Edward CRANEY's children all my personal effects. Exor. Charles BINNS Clerk of Loudoun and Samuel MURREY of Loudoun. Witness: Robt. WILSON, Thomas ADDAMS Senr., Benjamin HEATON.

Bk:Pg: 01:10059 Date: ___
Will of Samuel PUGH of Richmond Co. dated 5 June 1771. To son David PUGH negro wench Bess. To son Samuel PUGH negro wench Lucy. To daughter Sarah PUGH and daughter Mary PUGH my mare, all remainder of cash and household goods and furniture. My brother David PUGH, George HOW and John HOW as Exors. Witness: David PUGH, Hannah BOYED, James ROBERSON. [not signed]

Bk:Pg: 01:10060 – 01:10061 [top] Date: ___
Will of Jonathan PIKE of Loudoun dated 15 May 1788. To a daughter of William THOMAS Jr. and Mary THOMAS £5. To Henry TALBUT rest of estate and bonds that lys in Mr. William B. SEARS hands to him and his heirs. Henry TALBUT as Exor. Witness: Mo. THOMAS, Edward SMITH, Hugh TALBUTT. Proven 13 September 1790 by W. THOMAS & ord'd to be cert'd. Henry TALBOT as Exor. with £200 bond with W. S. BELT & J. STEPHENS as securities. Arthur SMITH, Moses THOMAS & Temple SMITH Apprs.

Bk:Pg: 01:10061 [bottom] Date: ___
Will of Martha BRIAN of Loudoun undated (weak in body). To son John HESS $16 that I lent him. To daughter Jane one gown and petticoat. To daughter Mary one gown and petticoat. To son Daniel BRIAN the whole of my money and goods when he is at age 21 to be left in care of Johnston CLEVELAND for use of Daniel. Witness: William YOUNG, Alexander YOUNG.

Bk:Pg: 01:10062 Date: ___

Will of Jonathan PIKE of Loudoun dated 14 May 1788. Same as page 01:10060.

Bk:Pg: 01:10063 [top] Date: ___

Will of Martha BRIAN undated. Same as page 01:10061.

Bk:Pg: 01:10063 [bottom] – 01:10065 Date: ___

Will of Rebecca BRONAUGH dated 13 June 1827. To daughter Sarah BRONAUGH slaves Dick, Sally his wife and their children Hannah, Nancy and Florida. To daughter Rebecca SKINNER my boy Matthew about 12y old. Slaves shall not be sold or in any way disposed of by the husbands of my daughters without consent of daughters. Sons-in-law Martin BRONAUGH and Usher SKINNER as Exors. Witness: John W. GRAYSON, Elizabeth PAYNE. Codicil of 13 June 1827: to daughter Sarah BRONAUGH my negro man Moses aged about 30y. Witness: Elizabeth PAYNE. Proven 8 October 1827 by Eliz'th PAYNE the subscribing witness & ordered to be certified. 9th Martin BRONAUGH one of the Exors. with $3,500 bond and security. 8 March 1830 Usher SKINNER qualified as Exor. with S. M. BOSS his surety and $1,000 bond.

Bk:Pg: 01:10066 Date: ___

Will of Jacob SKINNER of Loudoun dated 3 February 1820 (in perfect health). To be buried at direction of my present wife Sucky whom I appoint sole Executor. To wife Suckey the residue of my property after expenses except one iron pot. I leave her freedom at my deceased. Witness: Thomas PHILLIPS, David JANNY.

Bk:Pg: 01:10067 – 01:10068 Date: ___

Will of Marcy TOMKINS of Loudoun dated 4 June 1800 (in good health). To daughter Sarai ROWEN one large silver spoon besides what she has already received. To my youngest daughter Betsey all of my wearing apparel, bed and bedding, saddle, furniture, two spoons marked with a single T and pair of sugar tongs all of silver. To daughters Polly and Nancy each a feather bed with bedding, table and chairs, one silver table & six teaspoons. To sons Benj., Asahel and Jonah TOMKINS the house and lots of land where I now live to be equally divided, my son Benj. to have his share adj. the house I now live in together with the said house. Son Asahel to have his share at the upper end of the lotts and I purpose to build him a house thereon and if I depart before the house is finished I do charge Benj. to finish the same. Son Jonah to have his share in the middle betwixt his brothers and they assist Jonah in building a like house to that of brother Asahel to whom I give the colt he is now raising and to each son one silver tablespoon. Rest of estate equally to her three sons and not to let any of her daughters want a home while they are single. If any die before they are of age, their part divided among others. Son-in-law George ROWAN and son Benj. TOMKINS as Exors. Witness: John LITTLEJOHN, Monica LITTLEJOHN. Codicil of 7 April 1803 witnesses by John LITTLEJOHN, Monica LITTLEJOHN.

Bk:Pg: 01:10069 – 01:10071 [top] Date: ___

Will of Mary FERGUSON of Loudoun dated 28 August 1822 (low state of health). Negro men Humphrey and Isaac to be emancipated within 12 months after her death. Negro girl Charlotte now about 13 years of age shall serve my sister Charlotte LAYTON and her heirs until she arrives at age of 30y and at the separation of that time be emancipated; any of her heirs to serve until 25 years of age then emancipated. Negro boy Randal LAWSON about 13y of age be hired out until he is 17 years old then to be bound by Exors. to learn some trade as he may choose until he is 21y of age and then emancipated. To my brother William Barton HUNGERFORD of Kentucky and my two sisters Elenor FIFFE and Charlotte LAYTON both of Maryland sums from disposal of negroes and furniture. To sister Charlotte LAYTON bedding. To sister Margaret ONEAL of Maryland my shawl. To brother William Barton HUNGERFORD my half dozen silver tablespoons. To niece Ann FIFFE my set of silver teaspoons and sugar tongs also all my Chinea Ware. to my husband Amos FERGUSON all the residue of my household and kitchen furniture. Friends Abner GIBSON and John SINCLAIR as Exors. Witness: Stephen T. BURSON, Thomas KENT, Emily FERGUSON.

Bk:Pg: 01:10071 [bottom] – 01:10072 Date: ___

Will of John RHODES of Loudoun dated 14 April 1805 (weak of body)(. To wife Nancy RHODES all personal estate. Children Mary & Tholomiah RHODES. When Tholomiah arrives of age 18y he is free to act for himself. Wife to manage the children while they are minors. Wife Nancy RHODES as Ex'x. Father-in-law Robert RUSSEL to care and see the same performed according to his intent. Witness: Alex. INNESS, William INNESS. Proven 8 Jul 1805 by Wm. INNESS. Ann RHODES q'd. Ex'x. with $1,000 bond and Rt. RUSSELL sec'y.

Bk:Pg: 01:10073 Date: ___

Will of Dublin BISSOTT/BISSIT of Loudoun (at an advanced age) dated 15 August 1805. To wife Nancy 1/3rd of balance thereof. Six children – youngest daughter Rachel, son Jerry, four elder daughters Dauphany, Minty, Amy & Zilpah. Friends James MOORE & Thomas PHILLIPS as Exors. Witness: Asa MOORE, John BRADEN.

Bk:Pg: 01:10074 Date: ___

Will of James GILL dated 25 Jul 1767. To mother Elizabeth GILL negro girl Martha with rest of estate and after her death to his brother George GILL. Brother George GILL as Exor. Witness: Jas. LANE, John MILLER.

Bk:Pg: 01:10075 Date: ___

Will of Mary WEST dated 15 May 1777. To cousin Elizabeth ELLZEY daughter of my brother William eleven negroes (Pugg, Tom, Pase, James, Hannah, Simon, [torn off], Fanny, Hannah, Suck & George) and all personal estate after debts paid. To my sister Elizabeth HANCOCK a bed, cupboard, cattle, horse. William ELLZEY and Elizabeth ELLZEY as Exors. [no witness signatures]

Bk:Pg: 01:10076 [top] Date: ___

Will of Morgan HOGUE of Leesburg dated 27 November 1793. To wife Ann HOGUE all household furniture, wearing apparel & estate of every description after debts are paid. If wife dies to go to his mother Elizabeth HOGUE. Wife Ann as Ex'x. Witness: Geo. EMREY, Samuel MURREY.

Bk:Pg: 01:10076 [bottom] – 01:10077 Date: ___

Will of James RICE of Loudoun dated 29 October 1810 (weak in body). To wife Bertha my negro woman Cate during her life and after her death to be disposed of as the rest of my property. To my five children by my first wife (William, Leonard, John, Susannah and Jane) $5 each and all the rest of my property to sell and equally divide between my other five children (Jesse, Isaac, James, Sampson and Rebeckah) except 3a of land to my son James where his smith shop stands. Robert BRADEN and Charles BENNETT Jr. as Exors. Witness: Isaac VANDEVANDER, Joseph VANDEVANTER, John VANDEVANTER, David LACEY. Proven 8 September 1817 by James VANDEVANDER & o. certif'd. Robt. BRADEN & Chs. BENNET qualf'd. as Exors. $1,200 bond & sec'y given.

Bk:Pg: 01:10078 Date: ___

Will of James McNATHAN dated 16 September 1805 (weak in body). To George FOX an arithmetic book wrote by Nicholas PIKE, one d° named the assistant to James JEFFERSON. Wife Tabitha McNATHAN to have her bed and furniture, chest and wearing apparel. Rest of property to be sold and put in hands of George KILGORE to give to my wife as needed. George KILGOUR and Jno. JEFFERSON as Exors. Witness: George KILLGORE, John JEFFERSON, Thos. E. MINOR.

Bk:Pg: 01:10079 Date: ___

Will of Benjamin FULKERSON of Loudoun dated 5 December 1795 (sick and weak of body). To wife Allice £100 and £86. To my son Philip when he arrives at 21y of age £50. To son Josia £50. To daughter Sarah £50 when she is of age. To son Benjamin when he arrives at age 21 £50 and £20 towards his schooling. To son William when he arrives at 21y of age £50 and £20 towards his schooling. To daughter Anna £50 when she be of age and £20 for her schooling. Wife Allice as sole manager of estate as long as she remains my widow and not longer with assistance of Joseph CARR as Exor. Witness: Benj. BONHAM, Joseph BALDWIN, name in foreign language. Proven 12 April 1796 by Joseph BALDWIN & cert'd. Alice FULKERSON q'd. Ex'x. (liberty &c) £1,000 bond with Js. BALDWIN & Jno. RICHARDS sec'y.

Bk:Pg: 01:10081 [top] Date: ___

Will of Anne STEPHENS of Loudoun dated 3 September 1772. To grandson Lewis STEPHENS, to grandson John PRETSILL, to grandson Isaac PRETSILL, to grandson Frederick PRETSILL, to daughter Charity PRETSILL and her husband Isaac PRETSILL, mulatto girl Rachel JOHNSON. Witness: James GOFF, Martha MURSHITE.

Bk:Pg: 01:10081 [bottom] – 01:10083 [top] Date: ___

Will of Winniford SMITH of Loudoun (advanced in years and infirm in body) dated 9 August 1815. To son Charles SMITH negroes Silvey, Joseph, Bidwell, Eadey, Delphey and Edmond, all bedding, furniture & rest. To daughter Nancy SIMPSON negroes Rachel, Sary & Ellick, furniture given to her before. Witness: John W. COE, Edw'd. M. COE, Robert COE. Proven 11 August 1817 by J. Edward M. COE & o. to be certified.

Bk:Pg: 01:10083 [bottom] – 01:100845 Date: ___

Will of James M. KELLY dated 5 April 1794. To brother Edward KELLY all real estate in South Carolina and negro boy Sam, and all debt and rights in S. Carolina. To all my sisters equally divided all my rights to a part of my father's estate real or personal. To sister Margeret KELLY negro wench Rachael with her youngest child called Milly about 2y old and negro boy Jack the son of Rachael. To sister Mary KELLY mulatto wench Tamer with her child Anthony. To sister Mary Ann KELLY negro boy Nathan about 12y old and one other called Major about 4 or 5 years old. To sister Monica KELLY negro wench Jane and a negro boy Jack (cut off) about 10 years old. To sister Monika negro boy son of Tamer about 6y old born shortly after I left South Carolina. The net residue to brother Edward who I appoint Exor. Witness: M. HARRISON Jr., Rueben JENKINS, Mary KELLY. Proven 14 Jul 1794 by M. HARRISON Jr. & ord'd to be rec'd as to personal estate & cert'd as to real.

Bk:Pg: 01:10086 – 01:10087 [top] Date: ___

Will of William JACKSON of Loudoun dated 5 February 1782. Eldest daughter Martha, second daughter Mary, son William, wife Abigail (gets lease on 175a from George William FAIRFAX and all personal estate). If wife marries or dies then estate to be sold and divided among my children (John, James, Sarah, Ann, Richard and Febe). Wife Abigil JACKSON as Exor. Witness: Benjamin PURDUM, Elijah HOUGHTON. Returned to court 14 April 1795. John JACKSON as Admr. with £1,000 bond and James McILHANY and James ROACH his securities. 14 April 1785 Admr. with the will annexed granted to John JACKSON bond & sec'y. given. Recorded Liber E, folio 104.

Bk:Pg: 01:10087 [bottom] – 01:10090 Date: ___

Will of Osborn KING dated 9 December 1797 (weak and sick). Crop in ground to be sold to satisfy James COLEMAN Esqr. his salary and debts (to sell stock and furniture if needed). Sell all property to cover debts. Friend John BINNS as Exor. Witness: Pusey SMITH, John VARNES, Malchor STRUP. Proven 13 Jul 1801 by William WHALEY & ord'd to be filed. Proven by M. STRUP 14 Jul 1801. John A. BINNS ref'd to qualify as Exor. Administration with the will annexed granted John A. BINNS with £1,500 bond and Benjamin SHREVE and James HAMILTON his securities.

Bk:Pg: 01:10091 – 01:10092 [top] Date: ___

Will of Osborn KING of Loudoun dated 22 Jul 1797 (sick and weak of body). Estate equally divided among Leven HULLS & (John KING, Reubin KING & Osborn KING) sons of John KING dec'd & Smith KING. Friend John BINNS as Exor. Witness: Henley BOGGESS, Edmund ROACH. 22 September 1797 - Negro woman Cate should be free at my death. Witness: Malchor STRUP, John WATTER.

Bk:Pg: 01:10092 [bottom] Date: 14 May 1827

Sheriff summons O. DUNHAM to appear in court 1st day of June court next to prove the will of Hannah BATSON.

Bk:Pg: 01:10093 Date: 14 May 1827

Sheriff summons Oliver DENHAM to appear on second Monday in June next to prove the execution of the will of Hannah BATSON dec'd. Filed 14 May 1827 & sp'a iss'd. Proven 11 June by O. DENHAM & ordered to be certified. Wm. SWARTS one of the Exors.

qualified, $6,000 bond with Wm. ROGERS, Asa ROGERS and Jno. HOLMES as securities.

Bk:Pg: 01:10094 – 01:10095 [top] Date: ___
Will of Hannah BATSON of Loudoun dated 15 August 1826. Worldly goods to be sold and debts paid. Money to Wm. SWARTS' children. Balance between children of sister Phebe ROGERS & her brother James SWARTS. Nephew William SWART and Hugh SMITH as Exors. Witness: O. DENHAM. Servant woman Cloe to chose her master or mistress & no regard to be paid to the price.

Bk:Pg: 01:10095 [bottom] – 01:10096 Date: ___
Will of Benjamin OVERFIELD of Loudoun dated 24 March 1813 (weak in body). To wife Mary OVERFIELD farm animals and furniture. To eldest daughter Nancy LEWIS $71. To youngest daughter Sarah LEWIS $1. To eldest son Martin OVERFIELD $1. To second son Samuel OVERFIELD $1. To two youngest sons Peter OVERFIELD and John OVERFIELD $1. Remainder to wife. Wife as Exor. Witness: John H. BUTCHER, Elisha MALIN, Elizabeth MALIN. Proven 10 May 1813 by Jno. H. BUTCHER & o. cert'd. Mary OVERFIELD qualified as Ex'x with $500 and Silas REES & Lewis JURY sec'y.

Bk:Pg: 01:10097 – 01:10098 [top] Date: 5 February 1808
Settlement acct. of estate of Samuel WALTMAN. Numerous payments for debts. Widow allowed £12.0.0/year for 3 years each for raising 5 children. Allowance of £41.13.4 to widow as her dower for 5 years being the time the rents is credited. Totaling £427.14.7. Returned to Court 5 February 1808 by Josh'a DANNIEL, Timothy HIXSON, Cornelius SHAWEN.

Bk:Pg: 01:10098 [bottom] – 01:100104 Date: ___
At Court held 11 Jan [cut off] On motion of Preston HAMPTON who intermarried with Elizabeth CONNER widow & relict of Charles CONNER dec'd, ordered that William GUNNELL, James COLEMAN, William STANHOPE, Pierce BAYLEY & John ALEXANDER settle the administration account and divide estate. Division – Saml. CONNER (negro Cate & her child named Cate, Hannah, Peg, Rachel). Saml. to pay his sister Sarah WADE 50 Shillings. Dated 14 November 1797 by Wm. GUNNELL Jr., James COLEMAN, Wm. STANHOPE. Settlement account with Exors. Preston HAMPTON & wife Elizabeth beginning 1779. Examined by subscribers Wm. GUNNELL Jr., James COLEMAN, Wm. STANHOPE January 1796. Settlement account by Clator SMITH includes income from hire of negro Cate and negro Harry.

Bk:Pg: 01:100105 – 01:100106 Date: August 1809

Appraisal of estate of John OXLEY. Farm and household items totaling $232.15. Court order dated August 1809 orders John ROSE, William DULIN, Presley SANDERS, Isaac STEERE and Isaac LAROWE to appraise estate of John OXLEY.

Bk:Pg: 01:100107 – 01:100110 Date: ___

Inventory/appraisal of estate of John DAVIS. Farm and household items. Returned 8 Aug ___ by Peter OATYER, William LEFEVER. Sale list purchasers: John DAVIS, Elizabeth DAVIS, John HAVENER, Jonah POWER.

Bk:Pg: 01:100111 – 01:100112 Date: ___

Appraisal of estate of Henry OXLEY. Farm and household items totaling $442.16.

Bk:Pg: 01:100113 Date: ___

Inventory of John McILHANY the elder in possession of Rosanna McILHANY his widow. Old woman Jenny suppose to be 90y old, Dinah suppose to be 47y old, Winifred suppose to be 25 y old, Sarah suppose to be 23y old, Sukey suppose to be 21y old, boy named George suppose to be 19y old, girl Charlotte supposed to be 17y old, boy Peter suppose to be 14y old, boy Harry suppose to be 8y old, boy Aaron child of Sarah 4y old, girl Winifred child of Sarah 2y old, farm and household items, totaling $3,150.

Bk:Pg: 01:100114 Date: ___

Division of estate of Rosanna McILHANEY. To Hannah PARKER: Winifred & Sukey, cows, furniture. Sukey sold by John McILHANEY the younger. To Rachel WHITE: negro George age 19y, cows, furniture. To Robert McILHANEY: negro Peter aged 14y, horses, furniture. Heirs of Jas. McILHANY dec'd: negro Sarah with her 2 children, cows, furniture. Heirs of Mary McKEMIE: negroes Charlotte & Harry, cows, furniture. Signed Josiah WHITE, Abiel JENNERS.

Bk:Pg: 01:100115 – 01:100116 Date: ___

Inventory and appraisement of estate of Francis ELGIN dec'd made 3 March 1814. Negro man Harry (a blacksmith) and tools, negro Henry, negro Joe, negro Luke, woman Syrea and her infant son George, boy Adam, boy Sam, girl Rachel, girl Nancy, girl Harriet, woman Hannah & her infant child Hannah, old man Anthony, old woman Lucy, farm animals and items, furniture, negro woman Lott and her child Harriott (Mrs. THRIFT), negro woman Lydda and her child Daniel (Miss ADAMS), totaling $4,130.

Bk:Pg: 01:100117 – 01:100118 Date: ___

Sale bill 28 April 1815 of estate of ___. Purchasers: Jacob DIVINE, J. HOUSEHOLDER, John CASE, C. MILLER, Dan MILLER, Amos JANNEY, Aaron MILLER, John PALMER, Abiel JANNEY, Peter MILLER, Jos. FLETCHER, Wm. GARRETT, Nat. MANNING, L. ELLZEY, totaling $718.08½. Signed John GRUBB, Clerk.

Bk:Pg: 01:100119 Date: ___

Inventory (sale) of estate of William ENEAS. Purchasers: James HARROP, Phebe NICKOLS, William COHAGEN, Isaac NICKOLS, Samuel NICKOLS, James HOGE, George CARTER, Landen YONG [YOUNG?], Black Henry, totaling $37.32.

Bk:Pg: 01:100120 [top] Date: ___

Receipts of estate of Charles DUNKIN. Rev'd of Chas. DUNKING Exor. of Chas. DUNKING dec'd $22.45 in full of Elias LACEY execution 27 February 1812. Signed Wm. ROSE, constable. 6 March 1812 received of Charles DUNKIN Exor. of Charles DUNKIN $5.00½ for account of fees for services rendered the said Exor. on acct. of said estate. Signed BLINCOE. 23 October 1811 received of Charles DUNCAN Exor. of Charles DUNCAN dec'd $2 in part of an act again him. Signed Thomas ELLES.

Bk:Pg: 01:100120 [bottom] Date: 9 January 1815

I hereby renounce my claim of an administration on the estate of my dec'd husb'd. Charles POWELL. Dated 9 January 1815 signed Martha POWELL.

Bk:Pg: 01:100121 Date: ___

15 Jul 1808 - rec'd from Chas. DUNKIN in crockery ware & from Mrs. LACEY for the work of negro Ross $22.01 to be apply'd to executions in the hands of Wm. ROSE agst. Chas. DUNKIN. Signed S. BEARD. 10 June 1809 rec'd from Chas. DUNKIN £7.11.3½ principal int. & cost on two notes of Chas. DUNKIN Sr. this was paid by the hire of a negro & in earthen ware in the last year. Signed S. BEARD.

Bk:Pg: 01:100121 [bottom] – 01:100123 [top] Date: ___

Settlement account of estate of Josiah CRAVEN with Mrs. Eliz'h CRAVEN now Mrs. LUCAS Admx. Numerous debts totaling $1539.38 with interest from 1 April 1814. Leaves $632.46 with 1/3rd to widow and remainder to three children. There is one negro boy belonging to the estate which was not appraised and is now in the possession of the Admx. In pursuance of the order of the court made 13 March 1817 the subscribers have settled the estate, signed Jno. LITTLEJOHN, Presley CORDELL, Wm. AUSTIN. 15 August

1817 ret'd & o. rec'd. April 1818 ordered that this a/c be again ??? by the Comr. LITTLEJOHN.

Bk:Pg: 01:100123 [bottom] Date: 21 October 1811

Received of Charles DUNCAN £0.7.6 in full of my black smith acc't against Charles DUNKIN dec'd. 21 October 1811. Signed Levi DOUGLASS.

Bk:Pg: 01:100124 – 01:100125 Date: ___

Will of Leonard ANSELL of Loudoun (aged and infirm) dated 2 October 1804. Children Peator, Michael, Leonard, Melchor, Martin, Beckey, Catarine, Dorety, Susanna. Real and personal property to be sold and divided. Friend John STOUSEBERGER as Exor. Not signed. Witness: Enoch FRANCIS, Johan [foreign surname], Isaac STEERE. 16 January 1815 on hearing subscribing witness it is opinion of the court that will shall not be recorded. Whereupon Nicholas FRYE and Peggy his wife prayed appeal which is granted upon his giving bond and security on or before the next Court.

Bk:Pg: 01:100125 – 01:100126 Date: ___

Will of William SNIDER of Loudoun (weak and infirm) dated 12 June 1799. To son Jacob several horses. To Peter my mare. Rest to wife Catharine SNIDER during her widowhood and at her death equally divided between my sons and daughter (William SNIDER, Henry SNIDER, Jacob SNIDER, Peter SNIDER and daughter Elizabeth SHRY). Son William SNIDER as Exor. Witness: John VERE, John ETCHER, William DAWSON. 10 September 1799 W. SNIDER Exor. ref'd to take upon himself &c and Cath'e. SNIDER & W. SNIDER q'd. Admr. with $2,000 bond & G. KIPHEART & Eskridge HALE sec'y. Cath'e SNIDER renouncing her int'st. in s'd will & claims her dower acc'g. to law.

Bk:Pg: 01:100127 [top] Date: ___

16 January 1805 summons for George FEICHSTER to appear in court immediately on behalf of Leonard ANSELL against Jno. STOUTSENBERGER.

Bk:Pg: 01:100127 [bottom] Date: ___

I promises and oblige myself to pay Benjamin REDMON £7.10.4 for calve rec'd of him. Signed 13 September 1806 Chas. DUNKIN. Witness: Lawson LEGG.

On demand I promise to pay to Joshua SMALLEY $10 current money of Va value rec'd this 9th of November 1805. Signed Chas. DUNKIN. Witness: Thomas ODEN.

[no page 01:100128 or 01:100129]

Bk:Pg: 01:100130 Date: ___

DUNKIN vs SMALLEY receipt for $22. DUNKIN note to Jos'a SMALLEY £3.0.0.

Rec'd of Chas. DUNCAN Exor. of Chas. DUNCAN dec'd $27 for shooting two years at ten dollars and one at seven. Signed George ROUSSEAU.

7 April 1810 received of Charles DUNCAN $7.50 in full for execution against Charles DUNCAN dec'd. Signed James FRASHER.

Rec'd of Chs. DUNCAN Exor. of Chs. DUNCAN dec'd $107.38 for an ex'n Jas. ALLEN vs said DUNCAN dated 6 October 1810 signed Thos. N. BINNS DShff.

Received of Charles DUNCAN £2.10.10 in full execution against Charles DUNCAN dated 17 September 1810 by Wm. ROSE, Constable.

Bk:Pg: 01:100131 Date: ___

Jas. ALLEN agst HARRISON &c execution payments, etc. leaving balance due $14.48.

Sir I am indebted to Allen DAVIS one barrel of corn which I will pay to you in a very short time or the value in money, as it cost suits you in order to accommodate him. Signed Chas. DUNKIN. Addressed to Capt. Chas. LEWIS, 28th March 1806

Bk:Pg: 01:100132 Date: ___

On demand I promise to pay or cause to be paid unto Charles LEWIS his heirs or assignees £2.14.9 for value recd' as witness, dated 12th October 1805. Signed Chas. DUNKIN. Witness: Vin't. L. LEWIS.

Rec'd 14 Jul 1810 of Charles DUNCAN $8 in a/c of George HUTCHISON's execution. Signed Wm. ROSE.

16 Jul 1808 rec'd of Mr. Charles DUNKIN Exor. of his farther {sic} £0.8.7 in full of all act. due Andrew REDMOND dec'd. Signed B. REDMOND Exor.

Bk:Pg: 01:100133 Date: ___

To Miss Catharine DUNCAN you will take notice that on the first Monday in March next I shall proceed to state and settle the administration act. of Chas. DUNCAN dec'd with his Exor. agreeable to the order of the court made February 1812 at my office in Leesburg. Signed John LITTLEJOHN, dated 4 February 1812.

To Henry DUNCAN you will take notice that on the first Friday in March next I shall proceed to state & settle the administration act. of Charles DUNCAN dec'd with his Exor. agreeable to the

Court of Loudoun made 14 February 1812 at my office in Leesburg. Signed John LITTLEJOHN, dated 4 February 1822.

To Mason DUNCAN you will take notice that on the first Friday in March next I shall proceed to state & settle the administration act. of Charles DUNCAN dec'd with his Exor. agreeable to the order the Court of Loudoun made 4 February 1812 at my office in Leesburg. Signed John LITTLEJOHN, dated 4 February 1812.

Bk:Pg: 01:100134 Date: ___

To Benjamin DUNCAN you will take notice that on the first Friday in March next I shall proceed to state & settle the administration act. of Charles DUNCAN dec'd with his Exor. agreeable to the order the Court of Loudoun made 4 February 1812 at my office in Leesburg. Signed John LITTLEJOHN, dated 4 February 1812.

To Coleman DUNCAN you will take notice that on the first Friday in March next I shall proceed to state & settle the administration act. of Charles DUNCAN dec'd with his Exor. agreeable to the order the Court of Loudoun made 4 February 1812 at my office in Leesburg. Signed John LITTLEJOHN, dated 4 February 1812.

To Susanna DUNCAN you will take notice that on the first Friday in March next I shall proceed to state & settle the administration act. of Charles DUNCAN dec'd with his Exor. agreeable to the order the Court of Loudoun made 4 February 1812 at my office in Leesburg. Signed John LITTLEJOHN, dated 4 February 1812.

Bk:Pg: 01:100135 Date: ___

Mrs. Susanna DUNCAN you will take notice that on the first Friday in March next I shall proceed to state & settle the administration act. of Charles DUNCAN dec'd with his Exor. agreeable to the order the Court of Loudoun made 4 February 1812 at my office in Leesburg. Signed John LITTLEJOHN, dated 4 February 1812.

To Lewis GARDNER you will take notice that on the first Friday in March next I shall proceed to state & settle the administration act. of Charles DUNCAN dec'd with his Exor. agreeable to the order the Court of Loudoun made 4 February 1812 at my office in Leesburg. Signed John LITTLEJOHN, dated 4 February 1812.

Bk:Pg: 01:100136 Date: ___

On demand I promised & oblige myself my heirs Executors Administrators to pay or cause to be paid to Obed HARRISON his heirs or assigns the just & full sum of three pounds Virginia currency for value rec'd. 21 July 1798 by Chas. DUNKIN. Teste Jonathan BEARD.

Statement of vouchers No. 27 Stephen BEARD, notes totaling $96.30.

Statement of vouchers No. 28 Thos. N. BINNS, notes totaling $77.60.

Rec'd of Chs. DUNCAN eleven dollars in part of an ex'n Stephen BEARD vs Chs. DUNCAN dec'd & Chs. DUNCAN Jr., 20 September 1808 by Ths. BINNS D Shff for Benjn. GRAYSON Shff.

Rec'd of Chs. DUNCAN Jr. five dollars in part of an ex'n. Stephen BEARD vs said DUNCAN dec'd October 18th 1808. Signed Ths. BINNS D Shff for Benjn. GRAYSON Shff.

Also rec'd two dollars in full of S. BEARD's ex'n. of Chs. DUNCAN Jr. Jan 8th 1810. Signed Ths. BINNS D Shff.

Bk:Pg: 01:100137 – 01:100138 Date: ___

Settlement account for estate of Charles DUNKIN dec'd by Charles DUNKIN the Admr. Balance due the estate $159.79. Court order dated 4 February 1812. Signed by John LITTLEJOHN.

Bk:Pg: 01:100139 – 01:100140 Date: ___

Will of John HATCHER of Loudoun dated 10 October 1801. To wife Sarah HATCHER all estate rents profit and income during her natural life. To son Noah HATCHER the plantation whereon I now live. Devise all the residue of my estate to my four married children (Joshua HATCHER, Ann DILLON, William HATCHER and John HATCHER). Son Noah HATCHER and friend George TAVENNER Sr. as Exors. Witness: Joseph ROBERTS, Stephen KERRICK, Levi HOLLINGSWORTH. Proven 11 February 1805 by Jos. ROBERTS and certificed. Noah HATCHER qualified Exor. with $1,000 bond and Jos. ROBERTS and George TAVENNER securities.

Bk:Pg: 01:100141 – 01:100152 Date: ___

Top part of page appears to be a continuation of a will.

Note: the following will is extremely difficult to read. Transcription could easily contain errors.

I George William FAIRFAX late of the parish of Truro in the county of Fairfax in the state of Virginia but now of the city of Bath in the county in Great Britain Esquire being of sound and a disposing mind memory and understanding do make and publish this my last will and testament in manner following Imperious I resign my soul to Almight God in humble hopes of pardon for my many sins and in everlasting life through the merits of my saviour Jesus Christ and as to my body it is my will and desire that it be interred in a decent but private manner in the most proper and convenient plott near where I shall happen to die and as to my worldly estate after payment of my debts legacies and funeral expenses I give devise and dispose thereof in manner following that is to say I give devise and bequeath unto my affectionate wife [page 10042] Sarah FAIRFAX all that tract of land whereupon Giles COOK lives called Elk Wood on Elk Branch in Berkley (late Frederick) County in the said state of Virginia containing about one thousand one hundred acres together with the following negroes and mulato slaves named Colly, Abraham and Johnny, Mirbilla, Grace, Fanny, Betty, and Sukey with their issue and increase to hold the said tract of land with the several negroes herein before mentioned unto my said wife her heirs and assigns forever I give devise and bequeath unto her said Sarah my wife all those my plantations lying and being on Potomack river between Pohick warehouse and Dogues Creeks in the parish of Truro in Fairfax County in the said state of Virginia commonly called or known by the name of Belvoir together with the mansion house and all other erections edifices and buildings thereon and also all and singular other my lands lying between the said tracts as well those left me by the will of my late father as those purchased by me of Colonel Philip Ludwell LEE Messiours Hugh WEST, William BERKLEY, James HAMILTON or any other person whereasoever and also all my household furniture horses carriages cattle sheep hoggs tools utensils and all and singular other the goods chattels and effects together with all such negroes male and female with their issue and increase which shall be on the said Belvoir estate at the time of my death (except such as are herebefore or herein after particularly named and bequeathed) and also all in those my two several tracts of land called Shannondale and Piedmont chiefly lying in Loudoun and partly in Berkley (late Frederick) County in the said state of Virginia with their appurtenances to hold and the said several plantation tracts of land mansion house negroes and all and singular the several goods chattels and effects herein before mentioned until my said wife Sarah and her assigns for and during the term of her natural life and from and after her decease I give devise and bequeath the same until Ferdinan or Ferdinando FAIRFAX third son of Bryan Fairfax of Towlston in the said state of Virginia to hold to him the said Ferdinan otherwise Ferdinando FAIRFAX and the heirs male of his body lawfully to be begotten forever and for default of such issue and I give devise and bequeath the same unto the next brother of the said Ferdinand otherwise Ferdinando FAIRFAX and the heirs male of his body lawfully to be begotten forever and for default of said issue I give devise and bequeath the same to the Visitors of William and Mary College in the City of Williamsburgh in the said state of Virginia forever for the use of the said college. I given devise and bequeath unto my said wife Sarah all those my several tracts of land and plantations

[page 100143] on Shannandoah River with those in Berkley late Fredrick County in the said state of Virginia with the tract of West Chanse land opposite thereto and also all those several tracts of land adjoining the Valie of Berkley together with the following negroes namely Boatswain, Harper, Harry, Will, Gabriel, Bobb, Rachael, Venus and Clara with their issue and increase and also all my other negroes and mulatoes both old and young male and female (not herein before or herein after particularly named and bequeathed) to hold the same plantations tracts of land and negroes with their issue unto my said wife and her assigns for and during the term of her natural life and from and after her decease I give devise and bequeath the same unto the said Ferdinand or Ferdinando FAIRFAX and the heirs male of his body lawfully to be begotten for ever and for default of such issue then to my right heirs forever and for default thereof then I give and devise and bequeath to the Visitors of William and Mary College in the City of Williamsburgh in the said state of Virginia for ever for the use of said College and my will and meaning is that the several tracts of land called West Chanse and Vals of Berkley and the two several tracts of land called Shannondale and Piedmont with the slaves increase shall always hereafter be received? esteemed and taken as part of and go along with the mansion house estate called Belvoir for the better support of the possessor thereof for ever held. I give devise and bequeath unto my said wife all that my freehold Estate called Toulston situate lying and being in the parish of Newton Kyme near Tadcaster in the West Riding of the County of York in Great Britain and also all my estate plate & household furniture linen and china which I may have at the place of my residence at the time of my decease. To hold the said two several freehold estates at Towlson and Redness aforesaid with their and every of their appurtenances and all my right title and interest therein as also the several goods chattles and effects herein before last mentioned until my said wife and her assigns for and during the term of her natural life and from and after her decease I give devise and bequeath to the said Ferdinando or Ferdinando FAIRFAX and the heirs male of his body lawfully to be begotten for ever and for default of such issue then I give devise and bequeath the same to the next brother of the said Ferdinand or Ferdinando FAIRFAX and the heirs male of his body lawfully to be begotten and for default of such issue then to my right heirs for ever then I give and bequeath unto my nephew

[p. 10044] Lancelot LEE and that my tract of land situate lying and being near Winchester in Frederick County in the said state of Virginia containing about two thousand acres to hold the said tract of land with the appurtenances unto the said Launcelot LEE his heirs and assigns for ever. I give devise and bequeath unto my nephew William LEE all that my tract of land called Poplar Spring situate lying and being near James STRODES and Isaac EVANS's near ??? in Berkley (late Frederick) County aforesaid containing about one thousand seven hundred acres to hold the said tract of land with the appurtenances unto the said William LEE his heirs and assigns for ever. I give devise and bequeath unto my said two nephews Lancelot LEE and William LEE the following negroes namely Pompey and Will sons of old Pompey, Frank, Will and John son of Sylvia, Phebe, Nan, Bridget, and Tom son of Rachael with their and every of their issue and increase to hold the same to the said Lancelot LEE and William LEE their heirs and assigns for ever as tenants in common and not as joint tenants. I give devise and bequeath unto my nephew George LEE the sum of one thousand pounds current money of the said state of Virginia. I give devise and bequeath unto my niece Sarah HERBERT (late CARLYLE) the sum of one thousand pounds current money of the said state of Virginia. I give devise and bequeath unto the son and only child of my late niece Ann WHITING deceased the sum of one thousand pounds current money of the state of Virginia but if he shall prefer lands in lieu thereof than I give devise and bequeath unto the said son and only child of my said niece al that my tract of land in Prince William County containing about one thousand three hundred and ninety acres and in case he shall make choice and prefer the said tract of land in lieu of the said primary legacy and bequest of one thousand pounds current money of the said state of Virginia as aforesaid that then the said legacy and bequest of one thousand pounds herein before given and bequeathed shall be utterly void and of no effect but in case he shall make choice of and prefer the said tract of land then to hold the said tract with the appurtenances unto him his heirs and assigns for ever. I give devise and bequeath unto my sister in law Hannah WASHINGTON wife of Warner WASHINGTON Esquire the sum of five hundred pounds current money of the said state of Virginia besides the lands I gave her husband but in case the said Hannah shall not be living at the time of my death then and in that case I give devise and bequeath the said sum of five hundred pounds unto the eldest daughter of the said Hannah WASHINGTON that shall be living at the time of my death. I give devise and bequeath unto Mary BRAZIER (if she shall be living with my said sister at the time of my death) one annuity of twenty pounds per

[p. 10045] annum current money of the said state of Virginia for and during the term of her natural life payable half yearly by even and equal portions out of the rents and profits of the Shannondale and Piedmont estates and I do hereby charge the same with the payment thereof accordingly. I give devise and bequeath unto my Executrix and Executors herein after named all my lands whatsoever and wheresoever not herein before particularly mentioned bequeathed and disposed of and all my claim and interest thereon and also all that my one fourth part or share of and in the Bloomery Mills and the lands thereto adjoining and also all those my lotts in Towles (not herein before particularly mentioned bequeathed and disposed of) with all my claim and interest therein to hold the same and every of them and every part thereof to my Executrix and Executor herein after named in trust to sell and dispose thereof or of so much and such parts thereof as may be necessary to go in and towards payment of my debts legacies and funeral expenses and the expenses attending the execution of this my will (if any personal estate not herein before given and bequeathed shall be insufficient for that purpose). I give devise and bequeath unto my worthy friend Samuel ATHAWES late of St. Martin Lane but now of Abthurth? Lane Common Street Loudon Merchant one of my said Executors herein after named all that my tract of land containing about one thousand and ten acres situate lying and being in the Rappahannock Mountains in Fauquier or Prince William County in the said state of Virginia to hold the said tract of land with the appurtenances unto the said Samuel ATHAWES his heirs and assigns for ever. I give devise and bequeath unto my worth friend John MAUD the elder of the City of York one other of my Executors herein after named all that my tract of land containing about six hundred and thirty acres situate lying and being in Culpeper County in the said state of Virginia to hold the said tract of land with the appurtenances unto the said John MAUD his heirs and assigns for ever. And as to all the rest and remainder of my estate and effects real or personal of what nature quality or kind soever or wheresoever situate I give devise and bequeath the same after payment of my debts legacies funeral expenses and the charges attending the execution of this my will to and amongst my nephews and nieces by whole blood equally between them share and share alike as tenants in common and not as joint tenants and I do hereby nominate constitute and appoint my loving friends Robert CARTER, Nicholas WILSON, Miles CAREY, George WASHINGTON and Samuel ATHAWES Esquires and William MAUD Gentleman Guardians of the said Ferdinand or Ferdinando FAIRFAX and trustees for him in the management of the several estates and property

[p. 11046] bequeathed to him by this my will and I do hereby nominate constitute and appoint Sarah my wife Executrix and the said Robert CARTER, Nicholas WILSON, Miles CARY, George WASHINGTON and Samuel ATHAWES Esquires and John MAUD the elder and William MAUD Gentlemen Executors of this my will and do request that each of them my said Executors will accept as a small token of my friendship a gold ring and ten pounds Sterling each for mourning over and besides the said bequests in token the said Samuel ATHAWES and John MAUD herein before mentioned given and bequeathed to them respectively. And lastly I so hereby revoke and make void all former and other wills by me at any time heretofore made and witness whereof I the said testator George

William FAIRFAX have to this my last will and testament contained in four sheets of paper to the foot of this three first sheets thereof I have set and subscribed my hand and to this affixed my seal this sixth day of July in the twentieth year of the reign of our Sovereign Lord George the Third by the Grace of God of Great Britain France and Ireland King Defender of the faith ??? in the year of our Lord one thousand seven hundred and eighty. G. W. FAIRFAX (seal) Signed sealed and published and declared by the testator George William FAIRFAX as and for his last will and testament in the presence of us who at his request and in his presence and in the presence of each other have set and subscribed our hands as witnesses thereto. Alex'r. HAY & James MARSHALL & Alex'r. GRANT & Sarah FAIRFAX.

George William FAIRFAX heretofore of the parish of Truro in the county of Fairfax in the state of Virginia in North America but now of the city of Bath in the County of Somerset in Great Britain Esquire do make this codicil to my last will and testament bearing date the sixth day of July one thousand seven hundred and eighty. First I do hereby revoke and make void the devises and bequests contained in my said will to my dear and affectionate wife Sarah FAIRFAX and my nephew Ferdinand or Ferdinando FAIRFAX and to his next brother and the respective heirs male of my said nephews and otherwise as mentioned in my said will of all that my freehold estate called Towlston situate lying and being in the parish of Newton Kyme near Tadcaster in the West Riding of the County of York in the Kingdom of Great Britain and also of all that my freehold estate lying and being at Redness in the said County of York in the kingdom of Great Britain and also of all my plate household furniture goods

[p. 10047] and chattels which I may have at the last of willed and devised at the time of my decease. And I hereby give the said estate and plate household furniture silver and china in manner following (that is to say) I give and bequeath all my plate household furniture silver china pictures books and [smeared] and other liquors which shall be in my houses at Bath and at Writhlington near Bath or either of them at the time of my death and my chariot and all my houses unto my aid wife Sarah FAIRFAX for her own absolute use and benefit. I give and devise unto my said wife all those my before mentioned freehold estates situate lying and being in the said County of York and all other the freehold estate or estates in Great Britain where I may die seized or possessed (if any) and all my estate and interest therein to hold the same unto my said wife and her assigns for and during the term of her life and from and immediately after the decease of my said wife or other sooner determination of her said life estate I give and devise the same estates and premises to my friends Samuel ATHAWES of Saint

Martins Lane Common Street Loudon Esquire, Robert BURTON of ___ in the county of Lincoln Esquire and John MAUD the elder of the City of York Gentleman and Joseph BEEVER of Saint Martins Lane aforesaid Gentlemen their heirs and assigns for ever upon trust that they the said Samuel ATHAWES, Robert BURTON, John MAUD and Joseph BEEVER their heirs and assigns do and shall as soon as conveniently may be after the decease of my said wife sell the same either by public auction or private contract as they in their discretion shall think proper and I direct that the said Samuel ATHAWES, Robert BURTON, John MAUD and Joseph BEEVERS or the survivors or survivor of them his heirs or assigns shall be good and sufficient discharges to the purchaser or purchasers of the said estates and premises for the purchase money thereof nor shall such purchaser or purchasers be liable to see to the application thereof nor be answerable for the misapplication or misapplications thereof. And I give the said money to arise by this sale of the said freehold estates and premises unto my said nephew Ferdinand or Ferdinando FAIRFAX third son of my brother Bryan FAIRFAX of Towlston in the said state of Virginia to whom also I give the rents and profits which shall arise from my said freehold estates and premises from the decease of my said wife until the said sale provided he lives to attain the age of twenty one years for his own absolute use and benefit but in case he should depart this life under the said age I give the said money to arise by the sale and the said rents and profits unto my nephew Robert FAIRFAX his next younger brother the fourth son of my said brother Bryan FAIRFAX to and for his own absolute use

[10048] and benefit and in case Ferdinand or Ferdinando FAIRFAX shall not have attained his age of twenty one years or in case of his death under the said age my said nephew Robert FAIRFAX shall not have attained his age of twenty one years at the time of such said I direct my said Trustees to lay out and invest in their own monies the money to arise by such sale in government or upon real securities at their discretion and the interest or dividends thereof to accumulate until either of my said nephews who shall be so entitled to the said money to arise by such sale shall attain his age of twenty one years or when I direct such accumulation to be paid to such nephew with the money to arise by such sale and I do hereby authorize and empower my said wife at any time during her life by indenture under her hand and seal to grant leases of the said freehold estates and premises or at any part thereof for any term or number of years not exceeding twenty one years in possession and not in reversion reserving the best improved rent that can be obtained for the same without taking any fee for the doing thereof and so as the life or lives to whom such lease shall be granted be not thereby rendered dispunishable of waste. I do hereby revoke and make void the

devise and bequest contained in my said will to my Executrix and Executors therein named of all my lands whatsoever and wheresoever not therein before particularly disposed of and of all that my one fourth part or share of and in the Bloomery Towers not in my said will particularly disposed of upon the trusts in my said will mentioned and instead thereof do hereby give and devise the said lands the said one fourth part of Bloomery Mills and the lands thereto adjoining and my said debts in Towers and all other the premises set by my said will given and devised to my said Executrix and Executors and all other my real and personal estates and effects of what nature or kind soever in the said state of Virginia not otherwise disposed of by my said will and his Excellency George WASHINGTON of Albemarle County in the said state Esquire [also something small written above – now in the County of Fairfax in the said state of Virginia George NICHOLAS] and Wilson Miles CARY of Elizabeth County in the said state Esquire their heirs Executors and Administrators upon trust to sell and dispose of the said real estates for the best price they can obtain for the same and to apply the money to arise by such sale and also my said personal estate in Virginia in manner or following (that is to say) in the first place to secure thereout the payment of the sum of two hundred pounds per annum current money of the state of Virginia to be applied to the maintenance and duration or otherwise for the support of my said nephew Ferdinand or Ferdinando FAIRFAX during the life of my said wife and in case by the death of my said nephew Ferdinand

[p. 11049] or Ferdinando FAIRFAX his brother my said nephew Robert FAIRFAX shall become entitled to the property which I have before given to my said nephew Ferdinand or Ferdinando upon the decease of my said wife then the said sum of two hundred pounds per annum to be applied in like manner in the maintenance or education or otherwise for the support of my said nephew Robert FAIRFAX during the life of my said wife and subject to the said two hundred pounds per annum I direct the said produce of my said real and personal estates in the said state of Virginia so given and devised to the said George WASHINGTON, George NICHOLAS and Wilson Miles CARY to be applied in the payment of any debts which I may owe to any persons in America at the time of my decease and in the payment of the several legacies I have by my said will given to the several persons therein named in current money of the said state of Virginia which debts and legacies I do hereby charge upon my said real and personal estates in Virginia so given and devised to the said George WASHINGTON, George NICHOLAS and Wilson Miles CARY hereby expressly directing that no part of my real or personal estates in Great Britain shall be subject or liable to the payment of the said debts and legacies and all costs and expenses attending the same and the execution of the trusts hereby reposed in them the said George WASHINGTON, George NICHOLAS and Wilson Miles CARY I give the surplus which shall be then remaining of the said real and personal estates in Virginia unto and amongst my nephews and nieces of the whole blood equally to be divided amongst or between them if more than one and if there shall be duly one such nephew or niece living at the time of my decease then the whole to such only nephew or niece and as to my personal estate and effects in Great Britain (after the payment of my debts in Great Britain and funeral expenses) I give and dispose thereof as follows (that is to say) I give thereout to my dear wife three hundred pounds for mourning for herself and servants or for such other purposes as she shall think proper to be paid to her within one month after my decease. I give to my worth friend John MAUD the elder of the City of York Gentleman one hundred pounds over and besides the tract of land in Virginia which I have given him by my will. I request my very worthy and most esteemed friend the before named Samuel ATHAWES Esquire one of my Executors herein after named to accept of fifty Guineas as a small acknowledgment of the trust I entertain of his friendly attention to me and of my great regard for him. I give to my before named nephew Ferdinand or Ferdinando FAIRFAX my best gold watch and chain and seal. I give one years wages to each of my servants who shall

[p. 10050] have been in my service two years at the time of my decease I leave it in the discretion of my Executors to give or not to give mourning rings. I desire my worthy friend the before named Robert BURTON Esquire one other of my Executors herein after named to accept of fifty Guineas as a small testimony of my friendship and regard for him. I give to the before named Mr. Joseph BEEVERS fifty pounds as a token of my respect for him and as some compensation for the trouble he will necessarily have in this execution of my will as one of my Executors. All the rest and residue of my said personal estate and effects in Great Britain I give to the said Mr. Samuel ATHAWES, Mr. Robert BURTON, Mr. John MAUD and Mr. Joseph BEEVERS upon trust to lay out and invest such part thereof as shall not be invested in the publick funds at the time of my decease in such government or upon mortgage of freehold estates situate and being in Great Britain with liberty from time to time to call in change and alter such securities at their discretion and upon trust to pay the interest and dividends hereof unto my said wife during her life for her own use and the said residue of my said personal estate and effects in Great Britain or the stock funds or other securities in which the same shall be vested unto my before named nephew Ferdinand or Ferdinando FAIRFAX provided he lives to attain the age of twenty one years for his own absolute use and benefit but in case my said nephew Ferdinand or Ferdinando FAIRFAX shall depart this life under the said age then to give the same to my said nephew Robert FAIRFAX to and for his own absolute use and benefit and in case my said nephew Ferdinand or Ferdinando FAIRFAX shall not have attained his age of twenty one years or in case of the death under the said age my said nephew Robert FAIRFAX shall not have attained his age of twenty one years at the time of such sale I direct the interest or dividends of the said residue to accumulate until either of my said nephews so entitled to the said residue shall attain his age of twenty one years which I direct such accumulations to be paid in such nephew with the said residue and I do hereby declare that none of the persons in whom I leave by this my will reposes any trust shall be answerable or accountable for the acts receipts or defaults of the other of them but each for his own acts receipts and defaults only nor shall they be answerable or accountable for any involuntary loss which may appear in their respective trust estates and that the before named trustees of my property in America shall be at liberty out of the said property there and the trustees of my property in Great Britain shall be at liberty out of the property

[p. 10051] in Great Britain to repay themselves all such costs and expenses which they may respectively incur in the execution of the trusts hereby respectively reposed in them and in case any of my said trustees of my property in America shall depart this life before the trusts hereby reposed in them shall be fully accomplished I do hereby authorize and direct the survivors of them from time to time to appoint another person to be a trustee in the place and stead of such deceased trustee in whom jointly with the survivor of them I direct the said trust property shall be immediately vested to which new chosen trustee I give the same powers over the said trust property as if they had been originally appointed by this my will and so in the manner upon the deaths of all future trustees of the said trust property in America I direct the survivors of them from time to time to appoint new trustees of the said trust property so that there may be always the same number of trustees thereof as I have hereby appointed and so in case of any of my said trustees of my said property in Great Britain shall depart this life before the trusts hereby reposed in them shall be fully accomplished I do hereby authorize and direct the survivors of them from time to time to appoint new trustees of the said trust property in Great Britain in the place and stead of such deceased trustees as the same manner and to which new chosen trustees I give the same power in all respects over the said trust property in Great Britain as herein before mentioned with respect to the trustees of my American property. I do hereby revoke and make void the appointment contained in my said will of Robert NICHOLAS Esquire and heirs to be Guardians of my before named Ferdinand or Ferdinando FAIRFAX and trustees for him in the management of the several estates and property hereby bequeathed to him and also the appointment of the Executors of my said will therein named and instead thereof do hereby appoint my said wife Sarah FAIRFAX and the before named Samuel ATHAWES and Robert BURTON Esquires and Mr. John MAUD and Mr. Joseph BEEVERS Executors of my said will as to all my estates and effects in the Kingdom of Great Britain and his before named Excellency George WASHINGTON, Wilson Miles CARY and George NICHOLAS Esquire Executors of my said will as to all of my estate and effects in the United States of North America and I desire the said Mr. WASHINGTON, Mr. CARY and Mr. WILSON [NICHOLAS] to accept of fifty pounds each current money of the state of Virginia to be paid out of my property in Virginia as a small

[p. 10052] token of my respect and esteem for them and I declare this to be a codicil of my said will which in all their respects I do hereby confirm. In witness thereof I have to the four first sheets of this codicil set my hand and to this last sheet my hand and seal this twenty sixth day of February in the year of our Lord one thousand seven hundred and eighty seven. G. W. FAIRFAX. Signed sealed published and declared by the above named George William FAIRFAX and ??? codicil to his ??? will and testament in the presence of us who in his presence and at his request and in the presence of each other have subscribed our hands as witnesses. The words "in Great Britain" having been ??? ??? in his first sheet, John SPEED, Henry Dup???, Clifton GLOUCESTERSHIRE, O. CROMWELL, Essex ??? ???
3 March 1787

I desire that my worthy friend and relation Lord Hawke of Yorkshire would be kind enough to be one of my Executors. I do hereby appoint the said Lord HAWKE one of my Executors for my English estate real and personal. G. W. FAIRFAX. Signed and sealed published and declared as a codicil to the will of G. W. FAIRFAX Esqr. in the presence of Robt. BARTON of the City of Bath. Esq., John DURIL?, Thomas SHEAK? servants to the s'd. G. W. FAIRFAX Esqr.

This will was proved at London with two codicils the twelfth day of July in the year of Our Lord one thousand seven hundred and eighty seven before the right worshipful Peter CALVERT Doctor of Laws Master Keeper or Commissary of the Prerogative Court of Castlebury? lawfully constitutor by the oaths of Sarah FAIRFAX widow the relict of the deceased, Samuel ATHAWES, Robert BURTON Esquires, John MAUDE and Joseph BEEVERS the Executors named in the first codicil and the Right Honourable Martin Bladen Lord HAWKE the Executor named in the second codicil to whom administration was granted and to the estate and effects of the said deceased in the Kingdom of Great Britain they having been first sworn that is to say the said Sarah Fairfax, Robert BURTON and John MAUD by commission and the said Samuel ATHAWES, Joseph BEEVERS and the Right Honourable Martin Bladen Lord HAWKE before the Worshipfull George HARRIS Doctor of Laws and Surrogate of the said Commissary duly to administer.

Bk:Pg: 01:100153 Date: 11 February 1881 RtCt: 11 Oct 1881
William R. MERCER, Y. Douglas MERCER, W. C. MERCER, Jane B. McCALL, Mary M. BROGDEN, Emily J. MERCER, Carroll MERCER and John F. MERCER to Charles R. PAXTON, John W. WILDMAN, and Alfred STANTON. Grant with general warranty 1a lot on which the Belmont Church now stands in trust for the use, benefit and control of the Episcopal Church. [Only signature that appears is Mary M. BROGDEN.]

INDEX

Other Heritage Books by Patricia B. Duncan:

1850 Fairfax County and Loudoun County, Virginia Slave Schedule

1850 Fauquier County, Virginia Slave Schedule

1860 Loudoun County, Virginia Slave Schedule

Clarke County, Virginia Death Register, 1853-1896, with Birth Records, 1855-1856, Entered on Death Register

Clarke County, Virginia Marriages, 1836-1886

Clarke County, Virginia Marriages, 1887-1925

Clarke County, Virginia Will Book Abstracts: Books A-I (1836-1904) and 1A-3C (1841-1913)

Fauquier County, Virginia, Birth Register, 1853-1880

Fauquier County, Virginia, Birth Register, 1881-1896

Fauquier County, Virginia, Marriage Register, 1854-1882

Fauquier County, Virginia, Marriage Register, 1883-1906

Fauquier County, Virginia Death Register, 1853-1896

Hunterdon County, New Jersey 1895 State Census, Part I: Alexandria-Junction

Hunterdon County, New Jersey 1895 State Census, Part II: Kingwood-West Amwell

Genealogical Abstracts from The Lambertville Press, *Lambertville, New Jersey: 4 November 1858 (Vol. 1, Number 1) to 30 October 1861 (Vol. 3, Number 155)*

Genealogical Abstracts from The Democratic Mirror *and* The Mirror, *1857-1879, Loudoun County, Virginia*

Genealogical Abstracts from The Mirror, *1880-1890, Loudoun County, Virginia*

Genealogical Abstracts from The Mirror, *1891-1899, Loudoun County, Virginia*

Genealogical Abstracts from The Mirror, *1900-1919, Loudoun County, Virginia*

Genealogical Abstracts from The Telephone, *1881-1888, Loudoun County, Virginia*

Genealogical Abstracts from The Telephone, *1889-1896, Loudoun County, Virginia*

Jefferson County, Virginia/West Virginia Death Records, 1853-1880

Jefferson County, West Virginia Death Records, 1881-1903

Jefferson County, Virginia 1802-1813 Personal Property Tax Lists

Jefferson County, Virginia 1814-1824 Personal Property Tax Lists

Jefferson County, Virginia 1825-1841 Personal Property Tax Lists

1810-1840 Loudoun County, Virginia Federal Population Census Index

1860 Loudoun County, Virginia Federal Population Census Index

1870 Loudoun County, Virginia Federal Population Census Index

Abstracts from Loudoun County, Virginia Guardian Accounts: Books A-H, 1759-1904

Abstracts of Loudoun County, Virginia Register of Free Negroes, 1844-1861

Index to Loudoun County, Virginia Land Deed Books A-Z, 1757-1800

Index to Loudoun County, Virginia Land Deed Books 2A-2M, 1800-1810

Index to Loudoun County, Virginia Land Deed Books 2N-2U, 1811-1817

Index to Loudoun County, Virginia Land Deed Books 2V-3D, 1817-1822

Index to Loudoun County, Virginia Land Deed Books 3E-3M, 1822-1826

Index to Loudoun County, Virginia Land Deed Books 3N-3V, 1826-1831

Index to Loudoun County, Virginia Land Deed Books 3W-4D, 1831-1835

Index to Loudoun County, Virginia Land Deed Books 4E-4N, 1835-1840

Index to Loudoun County, Virginia Land Deed Books 4O-4V, 1840-1846

Loudoun County, Virginia Birth Register, 1853-1879

Loudoun County, Virginia Birth Register, 1880-1896

Loudoun County, Virginia Clerks Probate Records Book 1 (1904-1921) and Book 2 (1922-1938)

(With Elizabeth R. Frain) *Loudoun County, Virginia Marriages after 1850, Volume 1, 1851-1880*

Loudoun County, Virginia Partially Proven Deeds

Loudoun County, Virginia 1800-1810 Personal Property Taxes

Loudoun County, Virginia 1826-1834 Personal Property Taxes

Loudoun County, Virginia Will Book Abstracts, Books A-Z, Dec. 1757-Jun. 1841

Loudoun County, Virginia Will Book Abstracts, Books 2A-3C, Jun. 1841-Dec. 1879 and Superior Court Books A and B, 1810-1888

Loudoun County, Virginia Will Book Index, 1757-1946

Genealogical Abstracts from The Brunswick Herald, *Brunswick, Maryland: Mar. 6 1891-Dec. 28 1894*

Genealogical Abstracts from The Brunswick Herald, *Brunswick, Maryland: Jan. 4 1895-Dec. 30 1898*

Genealogical Abstracts from The Brunswick Herald, *Brunswick, Maryland: Jan. 6 1899-Dec. 26 1902*

Genealogical Abstracts from The Brunswick Herald, *Brunswick, Maryland: Jan. 2 1903-June 29 1906*

Genealogical Abstracts from The Brunswick Herald, *Brunswick, Maryland: July 6 1906-Feb. 25 1910*

CD: *Loudoun County, Virginia Personal Property Tax List, 1782-1850*

www.ingramcontent.com/pod-product-compliance
Lightning Source LLC
LaVergne TN
LVHW021450080426
835509LV00018B/2230
9780788449130